RESISTANCE
AGAINST
EMPIRE

Interviews by
Derrick Jensen

PM

ALSO BY DERRICK JENSEN

RESISTANCE AGAINST EMPIRE

Interviews by
Derrick Jensen

With gratitude to the
Wallace Global Fund
for their continued support.

The following interviews appeared in slightly different form in *The Sun*:
Kevin Bales, Anuradha Mittal, Ramsey Clark, Alfred McCoy, Christian
Parenti, and Robert McChesney.

Back cover photograph by Derrick Jensen
Cover and interior design by Stephanie McMillan
Edited by Theresa Noll.

10 9 8 7 6 5 4 3 2 1

LCCN 2009912458
ISBN 978-1-60486-046-7

PM Press
PO Box 23912
Oakland, CA 94623
www.pmpress.org

Printed in the USA on recycled paper.

CONTENTS

INTRODUCTION

Nothing comes free. This culture is based on converting the living ("raw materials," or "resources") into the dead: products for profit. This is as true of cell phones as it is of solar panels as it is of televisions as it is of cardboard as it is of F-16 aircraft. Raw materials always come from somewhere. And there are consequences in the taking of them.

The primary consequences are not mainly paid by those who use these products, much less those who manufacture them. They are pushed onto those who are stolen from and exploited. The empire uses violence (or the threat of violence) to obtain whatever it requires, from the lives and labor of human or nonhuman slaves to coltan, bauxite, and oil. Indeed, the central purpose of empire is the extraction of raw materials and exploitation of resources, and the displacement of consequences onto others.

This book explores many of the consequences of empire and the methods it uses to enforce its license to extract and exploit. Anuradha Mittal describes the effects of colonialism and global trade on food security. Juliet Schor, Katherine Albrecht, and Christian Parenti discuss some of the mechanisms of repression on the home front, as citizens at its center are overworked, surveilled, and imprisoned. J.W. Smith explains how empire begins in the monopolization of land and ends in a global economy based on total control.

These voices, together with the others in this book, comprise a strong indictment against the empire that holds our planet hostage to its ruthless appetite. The empire spares nothing, and no one, in the pursuit of its single, fundamental objective: profit. The first step in decolonizing ourselves is to expose its mechanisms and consequences. The next step is to resist.

J.W. SMITH

Interview conducted on
July 13, 2000, at his home
in Santa Maria, California.

Economist J.W. Smith has a trenchant truth to tell us: "an enormous share of our wealth is stolen." That theft begins with the monopolization of land by especially a few wealthy elites, and in addition all settlers, then quickly moves on to the monopolization of technology and labor. At first, people fought back against the thieves, but initial conquest has given way to laws structured to protect the "rights" of the thieves. The final step is the erasure of this history from our social memory paired with a concomitant mythology that condones the theft of the commons declaring any suggestion of a more equitable arrangement infeasible, inefficient, or impossible. We now accept monopolization as normal, and thus its harms—to the world's poor, to workers in the industrial world, and ultimately to the planet—are rendered invisible.

But beneath the gospel of private property is the heresy of truth, and Smith is one of its heretics. He argues that cities have always depended on the countryside for their sustenance—food, building materials, and other resources—and this dependence is backed by military power. People of the countryside are forced to hand over their resources to cities and are thereby forced into the position of having to buy goods rather than produce their own. In doing so the people of the countryside give up their economic independence. This process was extended to imperial nations and their colonies and has now encircled the globe in what Smith calls a "movement from plunder by raid to plunder by trade."

The final truth is good news: the last effect of monopolization is revolution. Smith has written, "Eliminating poverty is not philosophically complicated." It's simple: people in a given region need to regain control over their own economies. And they will fight for what is theirs. Once people get a "taste of freedom, it is very hard to take that away."

J.W. Smith holds a PhD in Political Economics. He has written six books on the elimination of poverty and war, including *Economic Democracy: The Political Struggle of the Twenty-First Century* (Sharpe) and *Cooperative Capitalism: A Blueprint for Global Peace and Prosperity* (IED). He is director of research for the Institute for Economic Democracy.

Derrick Jensen: You've written, "Eliminating poverty is not philosophically complicated." To do so, you've said, we would need to "eliminate the monopolization of land, technology, and finance capital, and equalize pay for equally productive work, both within internal economies and between trading nations." Can you comment on this?

J.W. Smith: Let's first talk about monopolization of land. If someone were born into our culture with the fully developed intelligence of an adult, but without our social conditioning, one of the first confusing realities she or he would face is that all of the land belongs to someone else. It's a crazy situation. Before this person could legally stand, sit, lie down, or sleep, much less gain sustenance, she or he would have to pay whoever owned that piece of land. Now it's one thing to own something that you've built—a chair, perhaps, or a table, or shoes—but land, air, and water are entirely different categories. They nurture life, are necessary to life, and were here before we were born (meaning they're not our creation). Depriving others—all living beings, not just humans—access to land is to have the ability to kill them. I don't know if this has been put more clearly than by Rousseau, who wrote, "The first man who, having enclosed a piece of ground, bethought himself as saying 'this is mine,' and found people simple enough to believe him, was the real founder of civil society. From how many crimes, wars, and murders, from how many horrors and misfortunes might not any one have saved mankind, by pulling up the stakes, or filling up the ditch, and crying to his fellows: 'Beware of listening to this impostor; you are undone if you once forget that the fruits of the earth belong to us all, and the earth itself to nobody.'"

DJ: That reminds me of that famous saying by the nineteenth-century anarchist Proudhon: Property is theft.

JWS: Having been so thoroughly acculturated, and having never experienced or imagined anything else, few people realize that all land ownership is nothing more than social convention; that is, that the huge timber and mining and real estate and oil companies and so on "own" their land only because we all agree—all have been taught to believe—that they own them. This social belief deprives others of their rights to what nature has endowed this earth.

DJ: Are you against all land ownership?

JWS: Not at all. I'm against this monopolization of land ownership that we all accept as seemingly natural. And this monopolization isn't that old, when you consider it in terms of human existence. Of course, most indigenous peoples do not believe in private ownership of land but rather view communally held land as a form of social wealth, something to take pride in, to take care of. Then, as Rousseau stated, along came civilization, with its basis in private property.

DJ: The word "private," by the way, comes from the same root as *deprive*, the Latin *deprivare*, because wealthy Romans walled off land for their own private use, depriving everyone else of access.

JWS: It didn't take long for the Romans to get around to doing that. At first all Roman citizens had inalienable rights to a homestead, with everything else held in common. But by the end of the Roman Empire only eighteen hundred men owned all of the "known world." Earlier the Greeks had tried the same thing: at one point only 2 percent of Greeks owned the entire empire. Today we see the same thing happening again: in 1974 the Federal Reserve estimated that 25 percent of all American citizens had no net assets. By 1988 it had risen to 54 percent. And of course today it's even higher. This inequality becomes clear when one learns that socialist Cuba has 85 percent home ownership ratio with no debt while America has 68 percent home ownership with massive debt. If one's debt is 85 percent of the value of the home, one only owns 15 percent of one's home.

DJ: How does land monopolization come about?

JWS: At first by conquest, and then by inequality continually being restructured into law. The powerful already understand the advantage of laws facilitating monopolization of land. And of course it is they who gain title to the majority of the land. The Greek aristocracy took it by force from the barbarians and from the peasants. The Romans did the same. Then after the collapse of the Roman Empire, in what is called the Dark Ages, peasants reclaimed their land. A belief in freedom and natural rights lasted for many centuries, until the church, nation-states, and powerful clans combined to wrest this land away from the people. Petr Kropotkin calls the slaughter of small landowners—hundreds of thousands of them—by the aristocracy the "birth of the modern state."

Once the land had been taken from the people, laws were passed to make the theft legal, and attempts to redress it were punishable by the full power of the state. Between 1760 and 1844, for example, nearly four thousand enclosure acts were passed in Britain. The result was that soon enough fifteen hundred families owned 90 percent of all the land there.

Once this monopolization of land ownership has been legalized, the next step is to attempt to erase our collective memory of social ownership. All major forms of discourse, from pulpits to universities to media outlets, tell us again and again that the sorts of communal mutual support means by which humans kept themselves alive until the rise of the state are infeasible, inefficient, damaging, or that they never existed. Those in power preach that their ownership of the world's wealth is efficient, just, and in the interests of the people. If we hear this often enough, and since we do not realize that an enormous share of our wealth is stolen form others, we believe it. Of course we are also unaware of the enormous wealth that is wasted maintaining a system that appropriates the wealth of the weak.

All of this has also happened in the United States. First the land was taken from the Indians by force. Then it was parceled out to the wealthy. Three quarters of New York was given to thirty people, and other lands were sold by the government to the rich at two cents per acre. Or they were granted to the rich on some excuse or another.

DJ: Ten percent of the landmass of the contiguous United States went just to the railroads.

JWS: In Texas, the government actually gave the railroads eight million more acres than it had the right to bestow!

And of course it was not only Indians who were killed, but non-Indian Americans, too, who attempted to resist. There were numerous bloody rebellions through the years—especially by farmers, who have historically been repressed—rebellions large and strong enough that they have constituted a threat to the land monopolies. But once land had been more or less legally granted to the elites, Americans were taught to believe that this was how our society should be arranged. Consider the fervency with which the gospel of private property is preached to all of us today.

DJ: What are the effects of the monopolization of land?

JWS: The entire wage economy, indeed, capitalism, is based on this monopolization. How do you get people to work for you at jobs they don't like? Well, there's always naked force. But that's expensive and would too closely resemble slavery. Since people need land to survive, if you can control their access to land, technology, and money, you can control them. You can force them to work for you at whatever wages you want to pay.

Another effect of this monopolization is waste. Whenever someone owns timber, oil, coal, or mineral rights, profit maximization requires maximum sales of these resources. Timber is clearcut, destroying ecosystems. And so-called sustainable forestry often only sustains profits, because the eucalyptus and other trees they plant to replace old growth are not native. They can be invasive species, water thirsty, and so on, and inevitably impact the land around the forests as well as those who depend on those forests. The tops are taken off of mountains to get the coal it is most economical to retrieve. Oil wells are put in wherever possible—and in the rush to extract oil, it's often wasted. Far more natural gas has been flared off because it doesn't make economic sense under the current structure to transport and sell it. Industrial agriculture leads to topsoil erosion, water depletion, chemicals in the water supply, and so on, while small family-owned farms are more efficient, and biodiversity-based agriculture is less costly to the environment. What I'm saying is that those who have title to resources inevitably sell them to make money, and that rush to make money wastes a lot of resources.

The same general dynamic is at work in the monopolization of technology. At one point all technology was owned by the group, to be used for the benefit of the group. But over time it has undergone the same shift as with land. The electric power industries form a good example of the effects of privatization of technologies: about 24 percent of the population of the United States is served by consumer-owned electric utilities. Even though much of this population is rural, and thus has a lower density, meaning higher per capita costs for the providers, privately owned utilities charge 42.5 percent more. This showed up vividly during the 2001 electricity crisis in California. Consumer-owned electric companies, instead of being threatened by blackouts, earned huge profits selling electricity to the private sector.

It's impossible to talk about monopolization of technology without talking about patents. Patent rights have a really interesting history. Did you ever wonder why payments on patent rights are called *royalties*? It's because kings and queens conferred patent rights to land and inventions on their favorites, with the understanding that the person so favored would rebate a share of the earnings—the royalties—back to the royalty. In short, the origin of patents is indistinguishable from the paying of bribes for the privilege of doing business.

And just as monopolization of land has been emplaced and maintained by force, so, too, has the monopolization of technologies. In the Middle Ages, for example, technologies for making and dyeing cloth were discovered that were more efficient than ancient hand methods. But the technologies were easily reproducible, so the question became, how could the cities maintain their monopoly on the technology? The answer is the same as with land. Throughout the fourteenth century regular armed expeditions from the cities went into outlying villages, breaking or carrying away looms and fulling vats.

DJ: Free trade in action . . .

JWS: Exactly: it was the birth of the modern market economy. But we'll get to that in a second. The point I want to make here is that just as was true with land, the technology monopoly that was originally kept in place by force is now kept in place by tradition. Today, because we're accustomed to it and unaware of society's (and our own) loss, we accept this monopolization of technology as normal. In fact, we are unaware that these monopolies even exist.

I'm glad you brought up the notion of free trade, though, because the grand movement that we would call the historical development of capitalism has really been the movement from plunder by raids to plunder by trade.

DJ: I don't know what you mean.

JWS: Well, the important thing to remember about those cities I mentioned a moment ago, and in fact about cities generally, is that they have no resources. They depend on the countryside for their subsistence. That's the way it is, and that's the way it always has been with cities. When those serfs came to town from the outlying villages and looked at looms and fulling vats, they said, "Well, we can do that." They already had the resources, the raw materials (which the cities *didn't* have). Back they went to their little villages, where they just produced their own looms and fulling vats, and whatever else was required. But if they were allowed to keep doing that, what would happen to the city? Down the tube it would go. If the city doesn't have that monopoly on capital, the city doesn't survive. So for several hundred years the rulers of the cities raided those countrysides, destroyed the equipment, and forced the people to sell their resources to and purchase manufactured products from the cities. That exchange between the world's powerful cities and their countrysides is still happening today.

Now, cities having conquered countrysides, the next step in this evolution was competition between different cities. If one city was able to take over the markets and resources of another city, that second city would go down the tubes just as fast as if the countryside was producing their own clothes and their own tools. So the cities go to war. We learned about the wars between Greek city-states in school, but no one ever told us why they were fighting. They weren't fighting for nothing, nor were they usually fighting over ideological or philosophical differences. They were fighting for their very living, as they perceived it. The winner got to control the resources and impose rules of unequal trade upon the one that lost the war. This same dynamic was then transferred to nations, and those nations became empires. Wars are fought over control of resources and trade.

The problem with war, from the perspective of the rulers of these cities, nations, or empires, is that it is very expensive. It's much more efficient to simply impose unequal rules of trade. Of course force of arms always stands behind those unequal trades, but plunder by trade doesn't cost nearly so much as plunder by raids.

DJ: What do you mean by plunder by trade?

JWS: History shows again and again that stronger nations, in order to feed their own market economies, have always denied weaker nations the tools to produce their own goods and forced them instead to trade their valuable resources for relatively cheap products they could have made themselves. Do you remember in the movie *Gandhi* when the Indian citizens were denied the right even to collect salt from the ocean, and were required by law to purchase their salt and other everyday staples from British monopolies? What many people don't know is that prior to the arrival of the British, India had an extraordinary economy, with thriving industries and a prosperous agriculture, even in such now-impoverished places as Bangladesh. It was crucial for the British to destroy that infrastructure in order for them to be able to get the Indians to purchase British goods: plunder by trade. China is another example. In 1800, the standard of living in China exceeded that in Europe. But because Britain consumed massive quantities of Chinese teas, and because the Chinese weren't interested in purchasing British goods, the British forced—at gunpoint—the Chinese to purchase opium, addicting a couple of generations of Chinese, in what was probably the largest commerce of the time in *any* commodity. When the Chinese resisted, 20,000 troops (including 5,000 Americans) went in to enforce the trade. Because the sales of opium exceeded the purchases of tea, Britain was able to maintain its own wealth. The United States cooperated in that suppression and practices similar suppressions yet today. Do you remember the infamous "open door" policies the United States imposed on Asian markets at gunpoint? Well, "free trade" is still imposed at gunpoint today; witness the dismemberment of Yugoslavia.

DJ: I still don't quite get it.

JWS: It's pretty straightforward: if you must conquer them by force, you do so. But you don't need to use force if you can absorb the other society's wealth by producing for that society what it should be producing for itself. The key is to keep them dependent on you, unable to develop their own skilled labor, innovations, industry, or wealth. What that means in practice is that you sell them as many consumer goods as possible, while simultaneously denying them access to technology, industry, finance capital, and, if at all possible, their own land.

This whole process is remarkably wasteful. I've always liked Lewis Mumford's description of what British colonialism did to both India and Britain: "The result was impoverished villages in India, hideous and destitute towns in England, and a great wastage in tonnage and man-power in plying the oceans between." It shouldn't come as a surprise that when a society buys from another society what it should produce for itself, there will be incredible waste in the process, and mass poverty especially in the economically defeated country.

But plunder by trade is expensive also for the winners. After the two big world wars of the twentieth century, the old empires of Britain, France, and so on were too broke to maintain control of the world—they no longer had the wealth or power to keep the world under control—so they pretty much handed the baton over to the United States. And we kept the world from springing free. That was what we called the Cold War. Most of us aren't aware that in order to maintain this control, the United States slaughtered at least twelve to fifteen million people. The public was aware of the overt wars but the government told the people this was to keep the world "free from communism." The real reason was the same as those cities eight hundred years ago: we don't dare let the countrysides spring free. If they're free, they'll use their resources for their own people.

DJ: I see how this is expensive for those in the colonies, but I don't understand how this plunder by trade is expensive for the U.S.

JWS: You're right, it is not as expensive for the U.S.; they gain wealth. But look at the waste. And the U.S. has to pay astronomical amounts to maintain and deploy the military. Imagine what could be done if even half the money the United States spends on arms were used for life-sustaining ends.

But no matter the costs, we have to keep doing it. The math behind it is really quite simple. There are only enough resources in the world for something like 20 percent of the world's people to be at the standard of living of the United States. That's a simple physical fact. This means that if the United States wants to maintain its position, it could *never* allow the rest of the world to industrialize in the same way. That's why we had to sink the Soviet Union. Now we're facing another large country out there, China. Twenty percent of the world's people, all in one spot. China must be contained. Those in power aren't stupid. They know they can't let China have industry or a standard of living compatible to that of the U.S. There are just not enough resources to do it. At some point in its development, China won't be able to increase its consumption unless we lower ours.

DJ: Let me know if I've got this straight. The central thing to understand this economic system is that nations do not have adequate resources, so in order to maintain their standard of living they have to exploit the surrounding countryside.

JWS: Where are Japan's resources? It's a pile of rock. Where are Taiwan's resources? Another pile of rock. Where are South Korea's resources? Where are Europe's resources? They consumed them or never had them in the first place. Europe consumes roughly fourteen times the resources that lie within its borders. There's the story behind Europe's violent history right there, in one sentence. America happens to have adequate resources, but not for current levels of consumption: with 5 percent of the world's people it consumes 28 percent of the world's resources. We consume far more resources than we have inside our borders. We're no different than those cities were eight hundred years ago.

DJ: And the effect of that on the colonies is obviously impoverishment . . .

JWS: Not only by direct expropriation of resources, but by unequal trade based on unequal wages. It's pretty interesting. Here's the math: if a worker in a dependent country gets paid one dollar an hour for labor that is equally productive to that of a worker in the imperial nation who gets ten dollars an hour, we normally think of that as a ten times differential in buying power. But it's far more than that. Say you're that worker in the Third World getting paid a dollar an hour to build toy cars, and can build one car per hour. Now, in the United States, I build a slightly different model of toy car, also at one per hour. I get paid ten dollars an hour. You in the Third World country have to work ten hours and produce ten cars to buy one of my cars. In that same ten hours I produce the same ten cars but I can buy one hundred of your cars. The wage differential, and thus the wealth accumulation potential, is exponential, not additive. That's why industry fights so hard to keep wages down. That's why they all want NAFTA, GATT, WTO, IMF, and the World Bank to impose these structural adjustments on the Third World. That drives down the price of labor and increases the wealth accumulation of the well-paid nation exponentially.

DJ: Can you describe some of the mechanisms for unequal trade? We hear all the time about the protests in Seattle, Quebec, and so on, but it's not always clear what people are protesting about. I mean, what could be wrong with free trade?

JWS: Free trade would be fine if it were truly free. But it's not. It's free trade so long as it all goes the way of the rulers of this country. If any country on the periphery got their act together and started gaining control of their own destiny, sanctions under those agreements would maintain the dependency status of that country. If you want to build up your country's economy, you invest in your education, roads, and industry. You support your industry. We've got massive supports of our agriculture and industry right now, though we claim we don't. They're massive, that is how America and every other successful country developed, and yet the developed world forces the opposite philosophy upon weak developing countries. If sanctions under those trade agreements don't work, then the U.S., with the support of other developed countries, covertly destabilizes those countries. If that doesn't work, the U.S. just invades.

DJ: How does the U.S. maintain its self-image as god's gift to the planet?

JWS: Put yourself in a government official's position. How are you going to step aside and say, "Well, we're not going to do it"? Could those city officials eight hundred years ago have stepped aside and said, "Let that countryside have their capital"? If you do that, the people inside the city will be hurting, they may even starve. Equal trade means just that, equal trade. These trades are horribly unequal and no American leader can push a truly honest trade policy. To do so would mean more wealth for the impoverished periphery, but their gain would be an immediate loss of wealth for Americans.

Ever since plunder by trade was established centuries ago, the world's powerful nations have been locked into it, and they can't break out. If any leader tried, the whole population would turn on them. It could work no other way. The population would be aware they were living well off someone else's wealth—after all they all were told the world depended upon them rather than that they depended upon the wealth of the rest of the world—and the government would be immediately toppled.

An entirely different system of commerce could have evolved if a society had a philosophy of equality of rights instead of a society built upon inequality of rights. There has been a battle for equality of rights throughout history, but those equal rights have never been attained.

Through taking control of their resources, the developing world could improve their quality of life. But since that would mean less resources and wealth for the elites in the developed world, weak nations must be denied control of their own destiny. Cuba is the best example of that. Cuba has health care and educational systems equal to the United States. And until the American embargo really started to bite, nobody went hungry in Cuba. Due to the embargo, any ship that touches a Cuban port cannot land in the United States, and any company in the world that does business with Cuba faces U.S. sanctions. That has ground Cuba to a halt. Yet that country is still doing far better than all the rest of Latin America and seems to be slowly gaining. Of course we will never acknowledge those gains, and the effort to destabilize Cuba goes on. Because if Cuba breaks free, gains control of its own destiny and its own resources, its standard of living will improve dramatically. The whole world will see that, and, boom, we'll have lost control of the world just that fast. That's why Patrice Lumumba had to die in the Congo, murdered by CIA agents who drove around with his body in the trunk of their car all afternoon. That's why the United States has had to overthrow democratically elected governments in Guatemala, Iran, Chile, and all over the globe. That's why the United States had to overthrow the democratically elected government in Indonesia and coax the new dictator to murder eight hundred thousand of his own citizens.

DJ: How do we in the United States keep ourselves oblivious to this?

JWS: The propaganda never ends. Think about the Cold War. We were told that there was a missile gap. A bomber gap. A window of vulnerability. All of those ended up to be pure fabrications. All lies told to maintain and bolster a military state. Now we're told we have to worry about so-called rogue states, or even individuals. Iraq. Osama bin Laden. North Korea. It's like James Madison wrote to Thomas Jefferson, "Perhaps it is a universal truth that the loss of liberty at home is to be charged to provisions against danger real or pretended from abroad." Think about that the next time some politician conjures up an image of foreign terrorists.

This propaganda is crucial to the maintenance of the system. We have to perceive ourselves as being the suppliers to the world. If enough people were to really internalize the understanding that the Third World is not dependent on the United States, and more broadly that *we* are not dependent on these monopolies, but that the United States is dependent on the Third World, and the monopolies are dependent on *us*, for resources to maintain the economy, people would rise up in a second.

DJ: How is this propaganda maintained? You can't hide the fact that the United States has invaded Latin American countries . . .

JWS: We always have a good reason for invading. We're protecting their own people, we say, from terrorists and dictators. Lumumba was a dictator, we said. Hell, he was the Congo's George Washington. We couldn't permit George Washington to be elected in the Congo, could we? The CIA and other intelligence services have wordsmiths who take everything that happens in the world and put it together the way they want the masses to understand it. I was talking once to Ralph McGehee, the former CIA operative who got a conscience, got out, and wrote the book *Deadly Deceits: My 25 Years in the CIA*. I asked, "Is it true that the U.S. orchestrates death squads all over the world?"

He said, "Of course." He also said, "I've never known the CIA to tell the truth to Congress." The CIA and FBI have huge infrastructures in place to spread disinformation and to destroy at least the reputations of dissenting organizations. There are hundreds of political prisoners in America's prisons who were placed there through the FBI's Operation Cointelpro, which was established specifically to destabilize rising political groups who may gain access to the media and thus access to the people, if they ever elected a leader to power. Our leaders, using words created by CIA wordsmiths, tell us that the people they kill in El Salvador, Guatemala, and elsewhere are communists and terrorists, and the corporate media repeats these stories word for word. But the ones they kill, besides poor farmers and Indians (not that it would be okay to kill communists), are teachers, professors, labor leaders, cooperative leaders, and church leaders— totally nonviolent people.

The biggest thing our country has to fear is democracy. That's why whenever we see one emerging we have to snuff it out and put in a dictator. In the 1970s the Trilateral Commission confirmed this with their report entitled, *The Crisis of Democracy*. They feared people were getting "too much" democracy.

There is something about this, though, that gives me great hope, which is the courage of the people who know that if they stand up their names will be put on death squad lists but they keep standing up. People are fundamentally good; they have to be conditioned by propaganda to do these violent, unjust things.

DJ: You've talked a couple times about waste, and about how wasteful the whole system is.

JWS: In some ways it all ties back to war. Because war is so destructive and wasteful, we had to build up a huge industrial capacity during, for example, World War II, although we could just as easily use any other war as an example. But what do you do with all of that industrial capacity when the war is over? By 1950, we'd replaced everything lost during the war, and we still had twice the industry it took to run the country. Any economist can tell you what that means: depression—immediately.

DJ: I believe that's called a crisis of overcapacity, isn't it?

JWS: In order to stave off depression, we kept that capacity going using the arms race. We built things that intentionally have no function in society. We built things just to keep the machines running. Because of the multiplier effect, if you shut down the military, suddenly 30 percent of the people in this country would be unemployed. So you have to keep those people employed, but they're really not doing any constructive work. What does a major in the army produce for any of us? Not food. Not clothing. Not shelter. And we have already demonstrated that these wars are really coming from the imperial centers. With the exception of efforts to break free, those wars are not coming from the periphery.

For that matter, how many people really produce anything at all? Seymour Melman wrote a whole book on that called *Profits Without Production*. He calculates that over 50 percent of the administrators of corporate America are unnecessary. They're not there to produce, but to intercept production.

Or think about planned obsolescence. It's central to our consumer economy. One of my favorite examples is light bulbs. Engineers have developed light bulbs that last twenty-five thousand hours. Yet manufacturers choose to produce bulbs with a span of a thousand hours. The reason is obvious: to get consumers to buy more light bulbs. But the labor that goes into them, in addition to the labor that goes into changing them, is all wasted.

Examples of this waste are everywhere. Junk mail. We get more junk mail than we do real mail. This unwanted and unneeded advertising consumes 90 million trees per year and millions of hours of labor, it creates junk, and it attempts to market products that for the most part people would never have missed had they never heard of them.

The insurance industry is notoriously wasteful. Each year the corporate insurance industry collects and holds in trust nearly $400 billion in premiums, employing over 2.2 million people. It's all a huge scam . . .

DJ: . . . stop the presses . . .

JWS: . . . because the insurance companies return to the public through claims only about half of what is taken in. Contrast that with Social Security, a public insurance fund, which employs only 63,500 people, and returns over 99 percent of what is collected back to its clients.

Some forms of insurance are less wasteful than others. Health insurance for organized labor in the United States, for example, returns about 87 percent of what is taken in. Since the interview, this number has fallen greatly. Individuals, however, can expect to get back less than 50 percent. Home insurance generally returns about 58 percent on what you pay in. Life insurance is extraordinarily inefficient.

The point is that it's all make-work. If we were truly interested in any sort of efficiency, in *really* meeting the insurance needs of our citizens, instead of making profits for the rich and make-work for so many, it could be streamlined, and billions of dollars and hours could be freed up.

We could make the same argument for our legal system. Not only are most lawyers unnecessary, they're often downright harmful: former Supreme Court Chief Justice Warren Burger claimed that 50 percent of practicing lawyers are incompetent and severely harm the rights of those they are supposedly defending. We could probably eliminate 80 percent of lawyers off the top without losing any productivity.

DJ: How so?

JWS: Divorce, accidents, and liability constitute at least 80 percent of all civil suits. Much of this could be resolved with no-fault insurance and simple forms. According to Jeffrey O'Connell and Andrew Tobias, the authorities on waste in these segments of the economy, if the public were just given access to standardized forms, about 70 percent of legal work could be eliminated. In New Zealand, the Accident Compensation Corporation oversees the claims process for liability. Injured people file claims, whether their accident happened at work, at home, or elsewhere, and compensation is provided fully and fairly.

Agriculture producing food that only destroys the agriculture economies of other nations, ever expanding health care systems that practice chemical and blade cures rather than preventions, monopolized patents, and monopolized finance: we could go through each of these one by one and show the extraordinary inefficiency of each. It's all wasted labor. And it's all central to our system.

DJ: How so?

JWS: It has to do with those monopolies.

Once you understand distribution through unnecessary labor as described in *The World's Wasted Wealth 2,* you can walk into an office building in any city, look at the plaques on the doors, and say, "Well, shoot, that doesn't need to be, that doesn't need to be, that doesn't need to be." Once people get their minds around this, they will see that a large part of our economic infrastructure has been built unnecessarily.

DJ: But how do we get around this unnecessary infrastructure? The government routinely subsidizes grossly destructive and immoral actions, things that don't even make any economic sense. The federal government subsidizes big timber companies to cut down the forests, when it could just as easily subsidize them to reforest. But that doesn't happen.

JWS: I would add the word "inefficient" to destructive and immoral. When the Europeans hit this country, the Midwest was covered with hardwood trees and we just burned them down. We probably burned down enough hardwood trees to build furniture for every family in the world. And the same thing happens now, both here and around the world. Australia has a forest of huge dead trees with rings cut around them to prepare the forest for burning, but the job was never finished. Capitalism, as it is structured, is inherently wasteful: it rewards the unrestricted consumption of resources, whether or not there is a productive end. That's why timber corporations clearcut. With no thought of the future, they run over thirty-year-old trees just because it makes that harvest easier. It's the same mindset that's caused us to burn down those hardwood forests. Someday, of course, those in power will say, "Whoops, I guess we shouldn't have clearcut or burned down all those forests."

Things will not, and simply cannot, change so long as we have these excessive rights of property. And if we do not change, we're going to hit a crash. The world simply cannot sustain this level of consumption.

The good news is that things *can* be restructured. The only way we can do that is by sharing, by restructuring for equal economic rights just as we are assumed to have equal political rights today.

DJ: What would your vision look like?

JWS: People talk about how war causes lots of technological innovation. Well, that's nonsense: what causes the innovation is money and hours being thrown at the problem. Just think if we threw the same sort of money at a sane, just, and sustainable economy? There would be *huge* changes overnight. Think how exciting it would be to live in that sort of society.

The important thing to remember is that we want to be here ten thousand years from now. How will we want to structure our society to make that happen? How will we want to use resources? How will we want to *not* use resources?

And to be honest, I don't think resource consumption is our biggest problem. I think we're going to poison ourselves with pollution long before we consume the planet. So, if we want to be around ten thousand years from now, we must alleviate pollution.

DJ: Everything you're suggesting is very sane. A big question I have, given what has happened and what continues to happen to everyone who opposes the monopolization of land, discourse, everything, is, how do we get there from here?

JWS: People don't usually change till disaster strikes and proves to them that what they were doing was wrong. That is what will certainly have to happen here. We have this whole imposed belief system in place to protect the power structure and its stolen wealth. So long as there are no major disasters—disasters that strike at the middle and upper economic classes—most people will continue to not know, and thus not care, about whom they hurt out there in the periphery. As long as there is food on the table, and toys to play with, most Americans aren't going to think about others' problems, and aren't going to listen to any discussion of it. Worse than that, their means of earning a living is tied to the system, so until the system begins to crash we can probably count on most people continuing to ignore the inefficiencies and injustices.

That said, we have to keep pushing so that when disaster strikes and changes must be made the knowledge is there to restructure the system to ensure economic rights for everybody.

DJ: How do you see this transition taking place through catastrophe?

JWS: It will always be tough: those in power are going to fight to retain those inequalities structured in law. And even if things were to collapse completely, there would be those who are tied into the system, who really cannot think any other way, who will back building up the same sort of system. That's all they know.

The change will be violent, no matter what. But if we don't restructure to create equal economic rights, we will continue to see increasing control of the entire world by a smaller and smaller number of people and organizations. Another way to say this is that we can struggle for change, fully aware of the violence this will bring about (including mainly violence by those in power against us), or we can accept fascist control of the world, which essentially is what we have now.

DJ: Define fascism.

JWS: Fascism is control of the country—or world—by industry and wealth, working covertly and overtly with the military to maintain that control.

DJ: What do we do in the meantime until the catastrophe? Just keep talking?

JWS: We have to keep trying to understand it. We all have to work as hard as we can to get this understanding and articulation out there as far as we can. Because when the system does crash—and it absolutely will some day; it always has in the past—that knowledge has to be there. People will have to know what went wrong in the past, so they don't make the same mistakes. Freedom is far more than political. One can have political freedom and still starve or freeze to death. People will have to know how to structure their society so all can gain true freedom, and true freedom means equal economic rights and equal rights to land.

KEVIN BALES

Interview conducted
on October 19, 2000,
by telephone.

"A lot of people would be surprised to learn that there's a very good chance they've got something in their homes that's got a link to a slave," says Kevin Bales. That's because there are at least 27 million enslaved people around the globe—more than came over on the Middle Passage. It is Bales's life work to see them all freed.

Bales's definition of slavery is simple: "a slave is anyone held by violence or the threat of violence, paid nothing, and used for economic exploitation." Though slavery is illegal everywhere, it is held in place by other institutions and social forces, from the IMF's structural readjustment programs to corrupt local governments. Economic growth, in particular, "is a disaster." Corporations are allowed to strip a country of its resources, like forests and metals, displacing millions of once self-sufficient people. Their poverty is precisely what makes them vulnerable to entrapment in slavery. And there are so many impoverished people that there is now an "absolute glut" of slaves worldwide. What exploiters are willing to inflict on "disposable people" is almost unimaginable, and yet it is going on right now: charcoal workers dying from burns, teenage girls driven psychotic by the abuse of prostitution.

Yet there is hope, in the determination of abolitionists like Bales and the brave survivors of modern slavery. Explains Free the Slaves, the activist organization that Bales founded, "We do not face the barriers previous abolitionists had to overcome—the laws are in place, there is no large-scale economic vested interest supporting slavery, and everyone agrees that ending slavery is morally right." Slavery can be ended. But we need to start by ending the comfort of our denial.

Kevin Bales is president of Free the Slaves and *emeritus* professor of sociology at Roehampton University in London. His book *Disposable People: New Slavery in the Global Economy* (University of California Press) was nominated for the Pulitzer Prize, and has been published in ten other languages. He is also the author of *Understanding Global Slavery, Ending Slavery: How We Free Today's Slaves*, and *The Slave Next Door: Modern Slavery in the United States* (all University of California Press). Bales is a trustee of Anti-Slavery International and was a consultant to the United Nations Global Program on Trafficking of Human Beings.

Derrick Jensen: You've written that there are more slaves alive today than came over on the Middle Passage. It may surprise some people to learn that slavery is not a horror confined to the past. What *is* modern slavery?

Kevin Bales: In many ways it's exactly the same as slavery two hundred, or three hundred years ago. It's still slavery in the sense that people are controlled by violence, are allowed no free will, are not paid, and are economically exploited. That definition of slavery applies whether you're talking about ancient Greece, Mississippi in 1850, or Los Angeles in 2000.

But slavery is also different now, in the same way that life is different now than it was in ancient Greece or antebellum Mississippi. We live in a global economy, and nowadays slavery is more globalized than it ever was before. It also tends at least sometimes to be more temporary, lasting for a more limited amount of time as opposed to generations. Perhaps most importantly, there are now a lot more people who are enslaved—there is an absolute glut of human slaves on the market—meaning that slaves have become very cheap, far cheaper than they've ever been in human history.

DJ: What is your definition of slavery?

KB: The word itself comes from the word "Slav," as in "Slavic peoples," by way of the Latin *sclavus* or *sclava*, meaning "Slavonic" (captive) because so many of the slaves in Rome were Slavs who'd been captured by German tribes. So far as the older definitions of slavery, I like Orlando Patterson's concept of what he calls the "social death" of the slave. Slavery, he says, is the permanent, violent domination of alienated and dishonored people. This definition, and the power relationship between slaveholders and slaves, can be broken into three components. The first is social and involves the use or threat of violence by the slaveholder to control the slave. The second is psychological and has to do with convincing slaves to perceive their slavery as actually being in their own best interests. The third is cultural and has to do with transforming force into a right of the powerful and obedience into a duty of the powerless, which, as Rousseau would have put it, ensures the powerful continual ownership. This latter means that the coercive power of the slaveholder is and always has been tied intimately to the coercive power of the state. The former can't exist for long without the latter. All that said, my own definition, the simplest one and the one I use most often, is that a slave is anyone held by violence or the threat of violence, paid nothing, and used for economic exploitation.

DJ: You use the word "slaveholder" as opposed to "slave-owner."

KB: In the past, slavery entailed one person legally owning another. But modern slavery is different. Slavery in terms of ownership is illegal everywhere, and there exists in the world no *legal* ownership of human beings. But there still exist many millions of people who are controlled and economically exploited by violence. The fact that the slaveholders don't technically own the slaves turns out in many cases to be in the interest of slaveholders, who now have all the benefits of ownership without the obligations and legalities.

DJ: You mentioned that slavery is globalized.

KB: One of the interesting things about slavery is that it was one of the first proto-globalized industries. The Middle Passage, for example, tied together three continents—Africa, Europe, and the Americas—and the profits made around that triangle shifted back and forth among these continents. It was very internationalist. But in the past, once slavery was in place, the slaves themselves and the products of their labor often remained local. Although slave-produced cotton was exported from the U.S., and slave-produced sugar was exported from Brazil and the Caribbean, to provide two examples among many, slaves often produced foods and other products for local markets. Today it's far more likely that the output of slaves feeds into the global market. For example, we know that there is a significant slave input in the cocoa plantations of West Africa. Now, chocolate is eaten all over the planet. Maybe 40 percent of the world's chocolate is tainted with slavery. Steel, sugar, tobacco products, jewelry; the list goes on and on. There are so many products tainted with slavery, and these products move so smoothly around the globe, that the global economy has smoothed the way to move slavery around the planet as well.

DJ: It sounds like everyone—or at least everyone in the industrialized world—probably has slave products in their home.

KB: A lot of people would be surprised to learn that there's a very good chance they've got something in their homes that's got a link to a slave. One of the difficulties in being sure, however, is that because the global market in commodities is like a money laundering machine, slavery can be very difficult to trace. Cocoa coming out of West Africa and entering the world cocoa commodity market, for example, almost immediately loses its label. If you're a buyer for Hershey's or another chocolate corporation, you don't say, "I'd like to buy six tons of Ghanaian cocoa." You just say you want so many tons of cocoa. When the cocoa is delivered at your factory, you can't actually tell whether this is Ghanaian cocoa, which might be free of slavery, or cocoa from the Ivory

Coast, which involved slavery. So you pass the slave-tainted product on without knowing, and the consumers buy it without knowing.

That's one thing I mean by the "globalization" of slavery. But I mean something else as well. It used to be that slavery tended to be virtually unique in every culture: the form of slavery you found in Pakistan wasn't the same as what you found in Thailand. But since the Second World War, slavery in different countries has become more and more alike. We're seeing a new, global form of slavery.

DJ: Could you talk about some of the differences between modern and older slavery?

KB: The kind of slavery most Americans hold in their mind is of course slavery as it was in the United States before the Civil War. That kind of slavery involved very expensive slaves. The average slave—average, not special—in modern money would cost about fifty thousand dollars. In part the high cost was because there was a shortage of slaves. It was hard to get good slaves, so they were expensive.

Today slaves are cheap, for a couple of reasons. The first is the population explosion; and the second is the pushing of large numbers of people in the third world into economic and social vulnerability. This means there are a lot more potential slaves out there. Now, factor in the third leg of the stool, the amplified ability to enforce slavery through violence, usually done by or with the approval of corrupt police or governmental officials, and you see how slaveholders can harvest so many slaves.

I'm not sure what the average price of a slave is in the world today, but it can't be more than fifty or sixty dollars. That's obviously a significant change compared to the fifty thousand dollars you'd have paid for a slave in 1850. And the low prices slaveholders put out for slaves influences how the slaves are treated. If you pay a hundred dollars for someone, that person is disposable. In gold mining towns in the Amazon, a young girl might cost $150. She's been recruited to work in offices there, but then is beaten, raped, and put out to prostitution. She can be sold up to ten times a night, and can bring in ten thousand dollars per month. The only expenses are payments to the police and a pittance for food. And if the girl is a troublemaker, or if she runs away, or if she gets sick, it's easy enough to get rid of her and replace her with someone else. It's not uncommon in some of these villages to wake up in the morning and see the body of a young girl floating by on the river. Nobody bothers to bury them. They throw their bodies in the river to be eaten by the fish. [Mineworker] Antonia Pinta described what happened to an eleven-year-old girl who refused to have sex with a miner: he cut off her head with a machete, then drove around in his speedboat, showing off her head to the other miners, who shouted their approval.

One of the reasons modern slavery is so pernicious is that people are so cheap they're not even seen as a capital investment: you don't have to take care of them, you just have to use them, use them hard, use them up, and throw them away. In this way people have become completely disposable tools for making money, an input to the productive process, in the same way you buy a box of plastic ballpoint pens.

So to sum up the differences between old and modern slavery, first, in old slavery legal ownership was asserted, whereas now it is generally avoided. Second, slaves were expensive, and now they're very cheap. Third, profits were historically very low: in the Antebellum South, slaves brought an average return of about 5 percent on investment. Now, agricultural bonded laborers in India generate more than 50 percent profits per year for their slaveholders, and rates of return of 800 percent are not at all uncommon for holders of sex slaves. Fourth, slaves used to be scarce, and now there is a glut. Fifth, because of the shortage, slave-owners used to maintain long relationships with their slaves, but slaveholders no longer have any reason to do so. Instead it is in their economic interests to dispose of them. Lastly, it used to be that ethnic differences were important: whites enslaved blacks, and not generally the other way around. Now ethnic differences are secondary to economic considerations.

DJ: How many slaves would you say there are in the world today?

KB: Around 27 million.

DJ: Your estimates are conservative, right? I've seen far higher estimates from, for example, the Anti-Slavery Society, and from the International Program for the Elimination of Child Labor.

KB: My definition—which is very rigorous—excludes a lot of really terrible things, which I agree are still terrible; I just don't call them slavery. Having just enough money to get by, receiving wages that barely keep you alive, may be called wage slavery, but it's not slavery. Sharecroppers have a hard life, but they're not slaves. Child labor is terrible, but it's not necessarily slavery. The United Nations talks about unfree forms of marriage as being a form of slavery. I can agree with that. But because most people conceptualize slavery as being an economic activity, I exclude it for the time being. I'm happy to accept it if anybody wants to push it, but for my own work I exclude it.

One other thing about those high estimates: I've of course seen them, too, and whenever I've tried to trace them back I was never able to find any solid underpinnings for the numbers. So a lot of those organizations, like Anti-Slavery International, have now adopted my numbers.

DJ: One of the things I found interesting about your book *Disposable People* was your hardheaded economic analysis.

KB: The works I found on contemporary slavery were full of outrage, which they should be, but they were pretty short on analysis. I felt there was a hole there, because while of course we should be outraged about slavery, we also have to analyze it to the point where we know how to make a start on ending it.

DJ: You break modern slavery into three forms: chattel, debt, and contract.

KB: Chattel slavery is the kind most people have in their minds, their historical memory of slavery, where people are owned, and there's a sense of legal ownership. In fact, in most places where you still have a kind of chattel slavery, it's not legal to own someone, but the system operates as if it were. You find that in the Arab countries, and Mauritania, and some parts of North Africa. But in fact that kind of slavery is fading away, because it doesn't really fit. It's still a kind of high expense slavery, and it needs a legal context.

Debt bondage, which is also illegal everywhere, is the most common form of slavery in the world today. It tends to be a little more flexible, and a little more adaptable to modern economics. A person borrows some money, and then pledges him or herself against that loan. The length and nature of the service are not defined, and their labor doesn't reduce the original debt. It's not even supposed to. All the work done by most of the people in debt bondage in, say, Pakistan or India, is simply collateral that belongs to the person who loaned them the money, until they pay back the debt.

DJ: I don't quite get it.

KB: Basically when you borrow this money, you and all of your labor become collateral. That's something most people in the West don't understand. They say, "Isn't this like a mortgage? I borrow the money and then I work to pay it back." But it's not like that. It's more like a mortgage where they say, "You borrowed this money, but all of your work, and all of the money that you pay in, doesn't pay back anything. It actually has to come from somewhere else."

That's the way it works with most debt bondage. *Some* debt bondage is supposedly about the work actually paying back what's been borrowed, but the reality is that it's almost impossible to pay back the debt. I've met families in India who've been bonded for four generations on an original debt. Grandfather borrowed thirty dollars, and great-grandson is still here working against that debt, because the debt has been passed on through the generations. One of the things that makes categorization slightly confusing is that if these people have controlled the family for four generations, well, now we're talking about chattel slavery. And in a sense it is kind of like chattel slavery because it's passed down through generations. But the rationale for the slavery is about this debt. That's all part of the subterfuge, the trickiness of it.

DJ: You said that debt bondage is common.

KB: There could be anywhere from 2 to 20 million bonded slaves just in India. Nobody knows. But, just to continue with the example of India, the tea you drink may have been picked by slaves. Jewelry, precious stones, bricks, timber, stone, sugar, fireworks, cloth, rugs, cigarettes: any of these might have been made by slaves. And even making and selling food, carrying and hauling, caring for animals, prostitution, proxy begging, and thievery may be done by men, women, and children who are bonded slaves.

The third major type of slavery is based on contracts. Contract slavery shows how modern labor relations are used to hide the new slavery. Contracts are offered that guarantee some sort of employment in a workshop or factory, but when the workers get to their place of employment they find themselves enslaved. This slavery is enforced by violence.

DJ: If you're going to use violence anyway, why bother with a contract?

KB: It's used as an enticement to get the worker to the place where he or she will be enslaved, and it's used as a way to make the slavery look legitimate: "See, you signed this contract saying you would work for me." The reality, though, is that the "contract worker" is a slave, threatened with violence, lacking any freedom of movement, and paid nothing. This is the most rapidly growing form of slavery and is most often found in Southeast Asia, Brazil, some Arab states, and parts of the Indian subcontinent.

Brazil forms a case study of some of the conditions that can lead to modern slavery. Brazil of course has a long tradition of slavery. Soon after the Portuguese "discovered" Brazil, the explorers realized how rich they could get growing sugar there for the European market. The indigenous peoples were quickly conquered and enslaved, but there weren't enough of them to supply the demand, and their numbers dropped quickly because of overwork and introduced diseases. By this time the Portuguese were already capturing slaves from Africa, and the trip to Brazil was far shorter than to the Caribbean or North America. Soon the national economy of Brazil was based on slavery: probably ten times more slaves were sent to Brazil than to the United States—somewhere around 10 million people. But because the death rate was so high on the sugar plantations, the slave population in Brazil was never more than half that of the U.S. The discovery of gold pushed slavery into the Amazon.

The international slave trade was abolished by 1854, but legal slavery continued in Brazil until 1888. At that point, slavery disappeared in the coastal regions, where there was at least a modicum of government inspection, but it's an open question as to whether it ever disappeared in the more distant parts of the country.

Brazil experienced an economic boom in the 1960s and 1970s, with predictable results: the military government courted foreign investors with promises of cheap labor and lax environmental and tax laws. Simultaneously the population exploded, the cities grew and filled, and mechanization drove even more people from the countryside. Pockets of poverty grew bigger and deeper.

DJ: I recall reading that a Brazilian general said around that time, "The economy is doing very well. The people, very badly." The figures I've seen for the period is that during Brazil's "economic boom" the number of undernourished Brazilians rose from 27 million to 72 million, of whom 13 million were so malnourished that they could no longer run.

KB: Things were not good. Then the military borrowed heavily to support nuclear and mining projects, and finally everything went bust in the 1980s. Hyperinflation wiped out savings, and servicing the $120 billion foreign debt crippled the economy.

Today, Brazil and its neighbor Paraguay have the greatest economic disparities on the planet. Fifty thousand Brazilians out of 165 million own almost everything, especially the land. Many millions have no land at all. And in the slums there are millions more landless and jobless. The austerity programs that brought the hyperinflation under control devastated the health and education systems.

There's one more piece we need to add to the puzzle in Brazil before we get to how the slavery works. In the 1970s the government and multinational corporations cooked up an immense tax avoidance scheme in which the government allowed multinationals—including such well-known corporations as Nestlé and Volkswagen—to buy blocks of hundreds of thousands of acres of federal land at ridiculously low prices. The companies then stripped away the native forest and planted eucalyptus . . .

DJ: . . . which is normally considered a noxious invasive species that from an ecological perspective should be eradicated everywhere outside its original range . . .

KB: . . . and the government allowed them to take the cost of the land and the replanting off of their taxes. The government promised to build a huge paper mill that was going to be fed by the eucalyptus trees. The mill never got built.

Brazil is also rich in iron. Now, to make steel from iron requires charcoal. The charcoal used to make steel for all the modern industries of Brazil, from cars to furniture, comes from denuded forests and slave labor. As you can guess, the forests of the region have been destroyed for charcoal, and now the frontier has moved a thousand miles away.

As the forests are used up near their homes, charcoal makers congregate in cities, hoping to find other work. They, along with millions of other displaced workers, find none.

That's where the contract slavers come in. Recruiters arrive in cities promising good work at good pay, and the unemployed leap at the chance. The recruiters promise good food and good wages. They promise that once a month workers will be driven home for a visit. Sometimes they even give out money so workers can buy food for their families. The workers sign contracts, and off they go. Along the way they stop at cafés, and the recruiters tell them to eat hearty because the meals will be paid for. When they finally arrive at the camp, they see that their working and living conditions are miserable. They see armed guards ringing the camp. The recruiter tells them, "You owe me for the cost of the trip, and for the food you ate, and for the money I gave your families. Don't even think about leaving."

DJ: They can't sneak past the guards?

KB: When the workers sign their contracts, the recruiters take from them their state identity card and their "labor" card. The former is proof of citizenship and essential for any dealings with the police or government. The latter is necessary for any legal employment. When an employer signs the back of a person's labor card, the employer creates a binding contract and brings the job under government employment laws such as minimum wage rules. Without that contract, workers have a hard time obtaining their rights. So even if the people dared to sneak past the guards, they're loath to leave without their identity papers. Besides, they're now a thousand miles or more from home, penniless, and in debt. And if they do get away, the locals fear them as outsiders. Without identity cards the police can arrest them as vagrants.

They live in concentration camps. And what those who run the camps want are slaves who have given up hope, who will do whatever is asked of them. They don't hesitate to use violence. At the same time, they want their captives to work hard, so they balance the terror with promises of payment, better food, better treatment.

The charcoal camps are their own little bit of hell in the forest. They each contain a battery of charcoal ovens, from twenty to over a hundred. The ovens are about seven feet high and ten feet wide with a door about four feet high in the side. Workers pack the ovens completely full of wood very carefully and tightly so it will burn down to charcoal, which is made by burning wood with a minimum of oxygen. The wood is lit, the door is sealed up, and then the burn is monitored, with vents opened or closed to control the oxygen intake. When the charcoal is ready the workers go inside the still-burning ovens to unload them.

I stood in one of the ovens for just a few minutes, and my head was swimming. I was addled. The coals burned through the soles of my heavy boots. Yet the workers in there were almost naked. Their arms and legs were covered with scars from burns, and many were confused when I spoke with them, almost as though their brains had been baked. They constantly hacked from the acrid smoke. If they survive long enough, many of them will contract black lung disease.

These contract slaves are usually controlled for somewhere between several months and two years. By that time the slaves are probably too ill to be of much use, and in any case, the forest in the region has probably played out, so the camp will have to be moved. It's better just to get fresh slaves.

DJ: You wrote that part of the reason there aren't more revolts is that the slaves are so honest.

KB: Absolutely. "We have a debt," they say, "so we're going to pay it off," even though that honesty is a one-way street.

Dishonesty feeds off honesty. The very rules of trust and honesty that guide most of these poor Brazilians in their dealings with each other are key to how the recruiters enslave them. Every one of the workers I met had a strong sense that the debts *must* be repaid, and that a person who did not do so was the lowest of the low. And this makes perfect sense. Imagine living in a rural village where you know all of your neighbors: your reputation is very important. If you have a reputation for dishonesty, then you'll have problems being a part of that community. You have to keep your promises and you have to pay your debts.

Slaveholders know this, and their manipulation of the slaves' honesty is far more effective than violence. Indeed, once the slaveholders use violence, the game is up, because the slaves realize they'll never be able to pay off their debt, and their sense of pride can no longer be used against them. At that point the violence may increase. Many workers have been threatened or beaten, and many know people who have disappeared.

DJ: Until reading your book, I didn't know that a lot of the environmental degradation in the Amazonian region is . . .

KB: . . . based on slavery.

It's the Wild West out there. Violence is used very freely. Violence is used to dispossess the people who live on the land, and then violence is used to enslave other people to destroy the environment.

Contract slavery works very similarly in Thailand, for example, except instead of men making charcoal, it is women being enslaved into prostitution. The story begins on the macroeconomic level in both countries. Joining the world economy has done wonders for Thailand's income and terrible things to its society. The economy's growth has been in many respects been a disaster, as the government has let corporations plunder the country of its human and nonhuman resources without forcing the corporations to give anything back. The forests are gone. The cities have been damaged. Pollution has increased. The lives of many of the people whose labor created this boom are grim. As in Brazil, impoverished families are presented with contracts that seem very reasonable: good work for good pay. And then away from home, the nightmare begins. Once the young women are used up they're discarded. And though the diseases are different, the slaves in both regions are usually ill when at last they obtain their freedom. Sex workers in some regions of Thailand have incredibly high HIV infection rates.

DJ: Let's talk a bit more about sex slavery in Southeast Asia. It gets more press than the other kinds of modern slavery.

KB: It does, although I have to say that sex slavery sometimes gets confused with sex tourism. A lot of people think those are the same thing, but they're usually not. The women involved in most sex tourism—and I say women, not the kids—have a certain amount of free will. They're not necessarily enslaved. Most of the enslaved women who are prostitutes in Southeast Asia are not used by tourists; they're used by local men.

The conditions of the sex slaves are really horrible. They may have been sold by their parents. They may have been broken in through beatings and rape. The rooms where they work might be five by seven feet, holding little other than a bed. They service ten to eighteen men per night. Violence—from pimps and from customers—is a very real daily possibility. Complaints from customers bring beatings from the pimps. In order to cheat the women and girls more easily, pimps wield terror randomly. Escape is nearly impossible. Slaves caught trying to escape are beaten, perhaps locked in a room for days with no food or water, then put back to work. Police serve as slave catchers, and abuse the girls at the station before returning them to the brothel. The slaves are often terrified of HIV. Their working life is maybe two to five years, after which they're worn out, and since the girls are so cheap—$800 to $4,000, with a daily profit to the brothel of $50 to $90—it is far more economically efficient to throw them away and find fresh girls. No brothel wants to take care of a sick or dying girl.

Once used this way, even if they do not have a death sentence from AIDS, the girls—young women—have often been shattered. They've done whatever it takes to adjust to a life of violence and being forced to have sex with fifteen men per day. Girls who've been freed and taken into shelters are often lethargic, aggressive, full of self-loathing, depressed, confused, or suicidal. Many have full-blown psychoses with hallucinations. Many feel they are unfit for anything else now. It's very difficult.

DJ: The testimony of Dina Chan moved me deeply. Can you talk about it and share some of her quotes?

KB: Her testimony is extraordinary. She's a member of the Sex Workers Union of Cambodia, and she originally gave the speech I cited in *New Slavery* to the First National Congress on Gender and Development in Cambodia.

"I want you to remember we are not 'problems,'" she said. "We are not animals, we are not viruses, we are not garbage. We are flesh, skin, and bones, we have a heart, we are a sister to someone, a daughter, a granddaughter. We are people, we are women and we want to be treated with respect, dignity and we want rights like the rest of you enjoy."

She had been lured into becoming a sex worker under false pretenses—one of those false contracts—and then she was locked into a pig slaughter cell and gang-raped. In the morning she heard the pigs screaming as they were being pushed into their pens. She said, "I knew what that feeling was like: I was no better than the pigs to these men; and they could have killed me. Something inside me did die, and I will never be the same."

When she got away from slavery, she began to work on her own as a sex worker. She said, "Some of you think I'm bad because I choose to remain a sex worker. My answer to those people is I think your society, my society, my motherland Cambodia, is bad because it doesn't give girls like me choices, choices I see are better for me."

"I think it is bad that my country allows men to rape young women like me and my sisters and go unpunished. I think it is bad that my society lets men seek and demand the services of women like me. I think it is criminal that we are enslaved to make money for the powerful. I think it is bad that my family are so poor and getting poorer because they can not survive as farmers with little resources which are getting smaller because more powerful people move them off their land."

She concluded, "I do not want to go to your shelter and learn to sew so you can get me work in a factory. This is not what I want. If I tell you that you will call me a prostitute. But those words are easy for you because you have easy solutions to difficult problems you do not understand, and you do not understand because you do not listen."

DJ: Within the strict constraints of her history, she's making a reasonable choice, but what about changing those awful constraints?

KB: One of the things I don't spend time on in my work, in part because—and call me a coward if you want to—it's so complex and so controversial, is the area of human trafficking for the purposes of prostitution. I do some work with those who are explicitly forced into it, whether they are in Cambodia, like Dina Chan, or in the United States or Britain. But the edges of that get very blurry. A lot of groups want to abolish prostitution completely, and a lot of others say we need to treat the non-enslaved prostitutes as sex workers, and make sure they have the dignity of a worker, the treatment of a worker. I've heard the abolitionists say, "No one chooses this. You can try to pretend people choose to be prostitutes, but to do that you must ignore the economic and social contexts, the brutalization, the sexism, the hierarchy." I think that's a very serious point that hasn't been necessarily worked out clearly.

DJ: Perhaps the place to start would be to do what Dina Chan asks, and simply listen to them.

KB: Yes.

DJ: Back to the larger question of modern slavery . . .

KB: I need to emphasize that all three of these kinds of slavery—chattel, debt, and contract—are identical in that violence is used to control the slaves, the slaves are paid nothing, they're economically exploited, and they can't walk away. These are just different mechanisms for enslaving people, and different rationales for the slaveholders to explain what they're doing. And like I said, the categories intermix. Four generations may end up being enslaved against a debt, turning it into chattel slavery. And some people will be given contracts, and then are told they have a debt.

None of these types of slavery are nearly as straightforward as the slavery that goes on in war—which is happening right now in Burma—where someone comes in with a gun and says, "Right, you. Come with me." In that case there's no debate about it, no rationalization. The more common types of slavery today are laced with rationalizations and mechanisms.

DJ: Sometimes the amounts of money for which people are enslaved, even for generations, are, by Western standards, trivial.

KB: It's heartbreaking. I talked to a farmer in India whose family had been enslaved for fifteen years. He didn't remember the size of the original debt, but he'd been able to get it down to about nine hundred rupees ($25 USD). The conditions under which he was enslaved guaranteed he would not be able to repay the whole thing. Another farmer had taken over his father's debt of twelve hundred rupees, or maybe $35, which was a lot of money to him. His father and grandfather had been bonded to the same master. Three years earlier he'd been able to get the debt down to two hundred rupees, or $6, but his family couldn't quite make it to the next harvest, and by the time I talked to him it was back up to about fourteen hundred rupees, or $39. And things were getting tougher, since his son had run off three years earlier, leaving behind a wife and daughter for him to support.

DJ: Didn't you just want to give him the cash in your pocket to get him out of debt?

KB: That's very tempting. And that might be one way to go. It's just that it wouldn't necessarily get them out of the system that enslaved them in the first place. It wouldn't necessarily give them the skills or the economic basis to maintain freedom.

You make a very important point, though, and a hopeful point, in that they could be freed for easily raisable amounts of money. But it's also true that if you look at what happened in the United States after the Civil War, where the government dumped two million people into freedom without any preparation, without any rehabilitation, without any kind of economic support or skills—I mean, they had skills and they knew how to work, but they didn't necessarily have the skills to instantly enter into the job market—you see that today we're still paying the price for that botched emancipation of the 1860s.

The point I'm trying to make is that when we talk about helping people into freedom, we have to remember that this freedom is just the first and not the last step. If you're actually going to help people have true freedom you have to not only pay their debts but help them to stand on their own feet.

It's also true, of course, that those debts shouldn't even be paid, because the debts are illegal in Indian and Pakistani law. There is no legal reason that anyone should pay these debts.

DJ: You said that freedom is just the first step. That reminds me of something you wrote in *Disposable People*, "Those who suffer new slavery, like the women in the brothels of Thailand, sometimes abandon any hope of freedom, but Baldev [one of the bonded workers in India whose debt was a generational holdover] was born without any hope." It seems important for slaveholders, or slaveholding subcultures, to eradicate hope in their slaves.

KB: It's crucial, because if they can close them in completely—psychically—they don't have to use violence. Violence is more expensive than destroying their wills.

DJ: It seems pretty clear that without at least a blind eye but more often the active participation of police and/or other levels of government, a lot of the slavery wouldn't be possible.

KB: That's absolutely the case. We have laws against it in every country, and some of the laws are really very good. The laws are good in India. But the laws suffer from a lack of enforcement, usually because at the local level, police or officials are on the take, and are active participants in the slaveholding process. Bringing an end to police corruption in the third world is a tall order. But there are steps that could be taken, having to do with professionalization, equalizing pay scales, and removing the tremendous temptation of money for a very low-paid police official. And of course also being very stringent about enforcing rules against police corruption.

DJ: It seems to me that the problem runs deeper than simply getting honest cops. Philosophers from the Ancient Greeks to the present have been explicit that civilization is based on slavery. Friedrich Engels, no fan of slavery, said, for example, "It was slavery that first made possible the division of labour between agriculture and industry on a considerable scale, and along with this, the flower of the ancient world, Hellenism. Without slavery, no Greek state, no Greek

KEVIN BALES

art and science; without slavery, no Roman Empire. But without Hellenism and the Roman Empire as the base, also no modern Europe. We should never forget that our whole economic, political and intellectual development has as its presupposition a state of things in which slavery was as necessary as it is universally recognized." Antebellum pro-slavery philosopher William Harper went right to the point: "Servitude is the condition of civilization."

KB: That certainly has been true. Slavery as we know it began when human beings started to settle and farm instead of wandering as hunters and gatherers. What we often call the beginnings of human history are also the beginnings of bondage.

DJ: Harper also wrote that without slavery, "there can be no accumulation of property, no providence for the future, no taste for comforts or elegancies, which are the characteristics and essentials of civilization." If we in the industrialized world want cheap steel, sugar, chocolate . . .

KB: Yes, it's not just about honest policemen, but also about honest law. If you have honest policemen who don't take bribes, but you've still got laws saying it's okay for the police to break up strikes, then the police are just following orders. But by breaking strikes, they are supporting the owning class.

It all gets complicated very quickly, because we're not just talking about police. We're talking about labor inspectors, safety inspectors, food and drug inspectors. If you protect people in the workplace, if you give them fair wages, then it becomes very difficult to make cheap goods. Cheap goods exist right now because human suffering has taken the place of high cost.

One of the ways to make a significant impact on world slavery is for consumers who are phenomenally rich compared to the rest of the world—like Americans and Western Europeans—to stop for a moment when they go to buy something and ask themselves how that particular item got so cheap. The inexpensiveness

59

of many items defies reason. I know we all hear that the items are cheap because of agglomeration, and effective marketing and all that . . .

DJ: I don't understand.

KB: You go to Wal-Mart, and see phenomenally cheap stuff made in China. Well, part of the reason the stuff is so cheap is that Wal-Mart buys huge quantities at huge discounts. And Wal-Mart and the other big chains have worked through their systems of distribution to reduce overhead all along the product chain. Okay, I believe that. Yes, they can sell stuff cheaper. But I suspect that these efficiencies and economies of scale don't account for all of the cheapness. There are a lot of questions about what happens in China, for example, in terms of slave labor in factories.

DJ: Is there a relationship between so-called free trade agreements and slavery?

KB: The end of the Cold War has seen an interesting shift in the rhetoric of the Western superpowers. They used to complain about how workers in many countries didn't have workers' rights, and the countries didn't treat workers fairly. When the Cold War ended, western governments stopped saying that, and said instead that free and open markets are what's important. The GATT and other "free-market" agreements are about opening markets. But none of those agreements contain provisions protecting workers' basic needs and rights, so-called social clauses. The WTO and GATT, according to GATT, are not required to consider the nature of workers' lives. This is a fundamental problem. There is an environmental clause in GATT, but the social clause has never been done. What this means is that we've established a context in which free trade can just step on people.

When you pump money into third world economies, the elite of those countries—the people who control the money flowing in, and the investment—

can operate as they please, because they don't have to answer to local law, and because there is no international law. If they choose slavery, that's okay, too. That's one way they can get ahead of other corporations or ahead of the industrial sectors of other countries. It makes them very competitive indeed.

DJ: Is there a correspondence between international debt and slavery?

KB: Absolutely. I coded up every country in the world by how much slavery they've got, based on my own archives, then ran a statistical analysis between that and the official figures on how much debt each country has as a proportion of its gross domestic product, and found a statistically significant relationship between debt and slavery, as well as between debt and trafficking. Half of the countries with heavy debt loads have slavery as a regular feature of their economies, as opposed to only 12 percent of those with a small amount of international debt. The citizens of almost three-quarters of the countries with large international debts are regularly trafficked into slavery in other countries. This is true for less than a third of those with low international debt.

DJ: That suggests one obvious way to reduce slavery.

KB: Forgiving the international debt would certainly help. We have to remember, though, that a correlation between the two—international debt and slavery—doesn't imply a causal relationship. But it certainly points in that direction. If the economy wasn't in shambles, and if people weren't being impoverished, then the people would be much less vulnerable. If you can reduce poverty, and reduce the shambles, you're certainly going to reduce slavery.

And of course we have to remember that the classic "structural adjustment" programs imposed on countries with large debt by the World Bank and International Monetary Fund decimate educational and health programs. Well, education is probably the single most powerful deterrent against slavery. If a government destroys its education programs to bring itself in line with programs imposed by the World Bank or IMF, one of the costs is that more of its population will be enslaved.

DJ: It seems that access to land is everything. To enslave someone dispossess them. To free them returns their access to land.

KB: Once people are already in the cities, enslaved to do low-grade processing—once you've urbanized them—you're past the point where access to land will help immediately. Certainly in the long run, they could regain food and other self-sufficiency. But there are very large numbers of people trapped in debt bondage in places like India, Pakistan, and Nepal, who desperately need access to their own land. The interesting thing is that laws in those countries for the most part provide exactly that, but it just never happens.

DJ: Why not?

KB: Corrupt judges, corrupt mayors, and corrupt administrators, for a start. At the village level, the landlords—the people who control the land—are usually also the local officials. And the police work for them. It's very hard to crack that.

Something big happened in Nepal this last summer, and no one in the West seems to know much about it. A very significant law against debt bondage was passed in Nepal last July 17: it frees people in debt bondage, wipes out their debts, guarantees them access to land, and so on. We were overjoyed at what we felt was a great victory. But within a month landlords began regular reprisals against bonded laborers to drive them off the land. They'd had these people basically as slaves for generations, and now they said, "Well, if the government forces us to give a little bit of our land to these people, we'll just get rid of them." So they go in with weapons and drive them off. Right now in Nepal you've got something like forty to fifty thousand internal refugees who were slaves until recently. Now they're just wandering the roads. The scale of this reprisal took the government completely by surprise. They weren't ready to get in there and enforce the human and now political rights of these people. The whole thing has gone topsy-turvy. It's almost like the beginnings of the Ku Klux Klan in 1866.

DJ: I was just going to say that. And the only thing that stopped the Klan was when the feds sent in troops in 1871. It's become pretty clear to me that that sort of violence breaks out when you have a privileged class whose specific privilege is being threatened.

KB: Sure. I'd assumed that people in the Nepalese government would have understood that people don't just roll over and say, "Okay, I used to be in power here, and now I'm going to give it up." It just doesn't happen that way.

DJ: You've written, "If we can't choose to stop slavery, how can we say that we are free?" That reminds me of a line you cite by Frederick Douglass: "If there are still slaves, how can you be proud of your freedom?" Can you comment on either of those?

KB: I feel positive about the challenge both of those statements make, particularly as it regards Americans. I recently spent eight months in America, until the end of August, and one thing that struck me was how positively Americans responded to the challenge of slavery, *when they knew about it.* But *that's* the crucial problem. As soon as people become aware, they say, "We've got to do something about this. We can't think of ourselves as free until we can crack this problem." So in some ways, I think one of the key parts of my job is to raise public awareness to the point where people say, "There are a whole lot of us, and we're going to do something about this." Every day that passes, more people become aware, and more people contact me or others to say, "I want to take up that challenge from Frederick Douglass. What do we do about it?" At the moment, to be honest, we don't have a whole lot to tell people, because there are so few ready answers.

There are, however, a lot of small answers. One of them has to do with attempting to discover what products are slave-based, and refusing to buy them. We're starting to do product tracing to help industries and consumers get out of the slavery business. Europe, for example, already has something called the Rugmark Campaign. Working from a tiny office with little funds, a group of activists proposed that people should look for a special tag on handmade rugs that would guarantee the rugs were not made by slaves. In order to earn the Rugmark, the producers had to agree not to exploit children, to cooperate with independent monitors, and to turn over one percent of their wholesale sales to child welfare organizations. Today, the German, U.S., and Canadian governments recognize the Rugmark label, and the biggest mail order company in the world, the Otto Versand Group, as well as many major retailers in the U.S., Germany, and Holland, now only import Rugmarked carpets. The carpets have thirty percent of the market share in Europe. Funds from Rugmark carpets have built and staffed two schools in India. We want to do Rugmarks for everything else, so people won't buy slavery.

Another small answer is for people to keep the awareness of slavery in front of their legislators. Two weeks ago I told people to tell their congresspeople to vote yes on the new trafficking law. That law passed, which is very good news.

DJ: Good laws are being passed, one in Nepal, and one here. So good things are happening.

KB: We're at the beginning of a movement. I can sense a wave mounting. I'm very happy to say—and I notice this particularly about Americans—that once people understand that real slavery still exists, their desire to stop it doesn't seem to be a passing fancy, where they comment on the problem, and then next week go on to another. They say, "This is terribly wrong, and we shouldn't forget about it until we see some progress."

ANURADHA MITTAL

Interview conducted
on January 24, 2001,
at Food First in
Oakland, California.

As I write this, many millions of Afghans are facing starvation. Meanwhile, the U.S. war against Afghanistan's Taliban regime continues to interfere with relief efforts. Every day the war goes on increases the risk of humanitarian disaster.

But is it fair to blame the U.S.? Doesn't the U.S. send food to hungry people all over the world, saving millions from starvation? Not according to Anuradha Mittal, former codirector of the Institute for Food and Development Policy, better known as Food First. She claims the U.S. contributes far more to world hunger than it does to feeding the world.

Food First (www.foodfirst.org) was started almost thirty-five years ago by Joseph Collins and Frances Moore Lappé, author of *Diet for a Small Planet* (Ballantine). Designed to be a people's think tank—more than half of its funding comes from individual donors—the organization seeks to establish access to food as a basic human right.

By now, we're all familiar with the images of hungry people in Ethiopia, Somalia, India, Bangladesh. But how has it come to pass that so many people are without food? Is it because there simply is not enough food to go around? Food First works to answer these questions, educating the public about the root causes of hunger and debunking the myths put forward by corporations and the governments that serve them.

Mittal, a native of India, once believed those myths. "When I was a little girl," she says, "I was taught in school that India had become independent through a long struggle, and that if we wanted to maintain our independence, the country had to move forward with development: building dams, investing in high technology. I remember how, before movies, we'd see a newsreel about the prime minister christening a new dam, after which they'd play the national anthem. I would get tears in my eyes."

When she went to college at the University of Delhi and became involved in student activism, she realized that she hadn't been taught the whole truth: "The dams were actually death centers that displaced millions from their land with no restitution, and those in power didn't care about the thousands of people they dispossessed or killed. I suddenly realized that human beings have a great capacity for making decisions that intentionally starve others. I wanted to know why." Mittal set out to reeducate herself.

As she is quick to point out, the problem of hunger is not restricted to India and other Third World nations. "The forces that are oppressing and colonizing people overseas," she says, "are the same forces that are oppressing working Americans in this country."

Trained as a political scientist, Mittal has extensive experience in food-related activism here in the U.S. and in the Third World. She's editor of two books, *America Needs Human Rights* and *The Future in the Balance: Essays on Globalization and Resistance* (both Food First Books), and has written numerous articles on global trade and human rights for *The Wall Street Journal*, *The New York Times*, *The Washington Post*, and other publications. Prior to coming to the U.S. in 1994, she worked with the Society for Participatory Research in Asia on issues of people's access to land and natural resources.

I spoke with Mittal on a warm day in January at the offices of Food First in Oakland, California. She was remarkably gracious, eloquent, and passionate. When I thanked her for her extraordinary work, she insisted that she merely plays a small part in a growing community of resistance.

Derrick Jensen: What is the scope of world hunger?

Anuradha Mittal: The United Nations estimates that around 830 million people in the world do not have adequate access to food. Numbers, though, distance us from the real pain felt by the hungry. Hunger is a form of torture that takes away your ability to think, to perform normal physical actions, to be a rational human being. There are people in my own country, India, who for months have not had a full stomach, who have never had adequate nutrition. This sort of hunger causes some to resort to eating anything to numb the pain: cats, monkeys, even poisonous roots.

When we think about hunger, we often picture dark brown faces, black faces, naked children with thin legs and bloated stomachs. This is the image of hunger the media have given us, but it is crucial to remember that hunger exists not only in Asia, Africa, and Latin America, but right here in the United States, the richest nation on earth. Thirty-six million Americans do not have enough to eat, and that number is growing. Nearly half of those lining up outside soup kitchens have one or more family members employed, but most of them are simply too poor to buy food. They are the people who scavenge in dumpsters outside restaurants. They're the schoolchildren who cannot pay attention in class because they did not have dinner or breakfast. They're people like Katherine Engels, a grandmother who testified at a Congressional hearing on hunger that she often drinks a cup of tea for dinner, then rolls up some white bread and eats it, because that gives her the sense that her stomach is full.

Hunger is a social disease linked to poverty, and thus any discussion of hunger is incomplete without a discussion of economics. Often, when we see a person asking for money for food, we think, why don't you get a job? How many of us realize that, of the people removed from the welfare rolls by welfare reform in 1996, only one out of ninety-seven will ever get a job that pays a living wage? At the minimum wage of $5.15 per hour, even if you work fifty hours a week, you earn little more than thirteen thousand dollars per year. There's no way a family living in a city could survive on that. They couldn't pay rent and put food on the table, to say nothing of clothes and other necessities.

If we're going to speak meaningfully about hunger, we need to understand the true causes of hunger. For example, hunger is not caused by shortage of food. According to our research over the last twenty-six years at Food First, the world's farmers produce 4.3 pounds of food per person, per day. This includes vegetables, cereals, fish, meat, and grains.

DJ: If there is enough food, then why is there hunger?

AM: People are hungry because they are too poor to buy food. There is a shortage of purchasing power, not a shortage of food.

Of the 830 million hungry people worldwide, a third of them live in India. Yet in 1999, the Indian government had 10 million tons of surplus food grains: rice, wheat, and so on. In the year 2000, that surplus increased to almost 60 million tons—most of it left in the granaries to rot. Instead of giving the surplus food to the hungry, the Indian government was hoping to export the grain to make money. It also stopped buying grain from its own farmers, leaving them destitute. The farmers, who had gone into debt to purchase expensive chemical fertilizers and pesticides on the advice of the government, were now forced to burn their crops in their fields.

At the same time, the government of India was buying grain from Cargill and other American corporations, because the aid India receives from the World Bank stipulates that the government must do so. This means that today India is the largest importer of the same grain it exports. It doesn't make sense, economic or otherwise.

This situation is not unique to India. In 1985, Indonesia received the gold medal from the UN Food and Agriculture Organization for achieving food self-sufficiency. Yet by 1998, it had become the largest recipient of food aid in the world. I participated in a fact-finding mission to investigate Indonesia's reversal of fortune. Had the rains stopped? Were there no more crops in Indonesia? No, the cause of the food insecurity in Indonesia was the Asian financial crisis. Banks and industries were closing down. In the capital of Jakarta alone, fifteen thousand people lost their jobs in just one day. Then, as I traveled to rural areas, I saw rice plants dancing in field after field, and I saw cassava and all kinds of fruits. There was no shortage of food, but the people were too poor to buy it. So what did the U.S. and other countries, like Australia, do? Smelling an opportunity to unload their own surplus wheat in the name of "food aid," they gave loans to Indonesia upon the condition that it buys wheat from them. And Indonesians don't even eat wheat.

DJ: In some South American countries, the governments grow and export coffee while their citizens starve. Have India and Indonesia begun converting agricultural lands to growing cash crops for export?

AM: Yes, as in other developing countries, we have seen an emphasis on export agriculture. Around three-quarters of the countries that report child malnutrition are exporting food. Remember the much-publicized famine in Ethiopia during the 1980s? Many of us don't realize that during that famine Ethiopia was exporting green beans to Europe.

In 1999, a UN Population Fund report predicted that India would soon become one of the world's largest recipients of food aid. The report went on to blame the increasing population for the problem. What it did not mention is that the state of Punjab, also known as "the granary of India," grows abundant food even today, but most of it is being converted into dog and cat food for Europe. Nor did the report mention that the neighboring state of Haryana, also traditionally a fertile agricultural state, is today one of the world leaders in growing tulips for export. Increasingly, countries like India are polluting their air, earth, and water to grow products for the Western market instead of growing food to feed their own people. Prime agricultural lands are being poisoned to meet the needs of the consumers in the West, and the money the consumers spend does not reach the majority of the working poor in the Third World.

DJ: I'm not sure it's Westerners' *needs* that are being met. More like their desires.

AM: Yes, luxuries are being construed as necessities, and freedom has come to mean the ability to choose from twenty different brands of toothpaste.

DJ: You've mentioned U.S. aid a few times. What's wrong with U.S. aid? I mean, isn't it commendable that we're willing to help out?

AM: I hear that a lot. I've been on radio talk shows where people have called in to accuse me of being arrogant and ungrateful: "Here we are, sending your people food aid, and you just complain!" I wish it were true that U.S. aid came from a generosity of spirit, but it has always been a political tool used to control the behavior of Third World countries, to forge dubious alliances, and to buy cooperation during the Cold War. With the end of the Cold War, aid turned into a scheme for finding new markets for U.S. agribusiness, and now for dumping foods containing genetically modified organisms (GMOs), which are being rejected by consumers in the West because we know so little about their long-term effects on humans and the environment.

But the deeper issue here has to do with the fact that food aid is not usually free. It is often loaned, albeit at a low interest rate. When the U.S. sent wheat to Indonesia during the 1999 crisis, it was a loan to be paid back over a twenty-five-year period. In this manner, food aid has helped the U.S. take over grain markets in India, Nigeria, Korea, and elsewhere.

I don't entirely reject the notion of food aid. Although I think that most countries can be food self-sufficient, there might be a few that need assistance. But aid has to follow certain principles. First, the food should be delivered when the people need it: i.e., right away. Second, it should not be used as a political tool, as in North Korea, where famine was allowed to bring the country to its knees before food assistance was provided. Third, the food should be procured locally or regionally, insofar as possible. And fourth, it should be culturally sensitive: the aid should consist of food that the people actually eat, and not just what a donor country wants to dump.

Having said this, let's look at the case of Somalia and Ethiopia in the 1980s. In this case, the food aid arrived very late, after the rains had already settled in and crops were ready in the fields. And the food was procured from big transnational agribusinesses in Canada and America. Local Ethiopian farmers were deprived of their livelihoods because cheap food was dumped onto the market at prices far below what the farmers could afford to match. In this instance, the food aid should have been sent earlier, and it should have been procured from neighboring countries, thereby supporting regional economies. That would have been real assistance.

I don't think it's too much to say that destroying local agricultural infrastructures is a central function of food aid. Once these local farmers have been driven out of business, the people of the region are dependent on the West for survival.

DJ: You mentioned GMOs. How does biotechnology fit into all of this?

AM: The big chemical companies want to increase their control over the world food supply by marketing genetically engineered crops, but consumers in the West are leery of GMOs. So, in 2000, the U.S. Congress approved a budget that included an estimated $30 million to promote biotechnology in the Third World. Seven million dollars of this was part of a deal between the U.S. and the Philippines to promote biotechnology as a means to achieve "food security." Money has also gone to support biotech research at American universities, and some of it went to help Third World and Eastern European governments encourage their regulatory agencies to approve the use of genetically modified food products. So regulatory agencies in the U.S., which have been asleep at the wheel on the issue of GMOs, will now train the regulatory agencies of the developing world.

DJ: That presumes that the agencies' purpose really is to regulate, as opposed to providing the illusion of regulation.

AM: Either way, the regulatory agencies have completely failed to protect American consumers. One example would be the StarLink incident, where genetically modified corn not meant for human consumption found its way into food. This mistake was not discovered by government agencies but by the Gene Food Action Alert Coalition, a civic organization that had the corn tested in a private lab. A month later, after initial denials, the Food and Drug Administration (FDA) finally acknowledged that a mistake had been made.

I could provide hundreds of examples of the incompetence of regulatory agencies or their outright capture by the industries they purport to oversee. It's a joke to think the regulatory agencies in this country are going to train agencies in developing countries.

At the same time, the U.S. is already sending genetically modified food to Third World nations without the consent of people there. In late 1999 and early 2000, when the Indian state of Orissa was hit by floods, the U.S. sent food aid containing GMOs. The Indian government was not told that the food had been modified. Mozambique, the Philippines, Bolivia, and many other nations have received similarly tainted shipments of food aid. More recently, when Sri Lanka adopted progressive legislation banning imports of genetically modified foods, it was threatened by the U.S., and pressure has since been put on the government to remove the restrictions.

The implication behind this is that hungry people in the Third World have no right to choose, or rather they have two choices: they can either die of hunger— often the result of decisions made by multilateral agencies with their offices in

D.C., Geneva, or Brussels—or they can take the unknown health risks associated with genetically modified crops. That's disgusting and racist.

I am deeply disturbed by the way hunger has been used to promote biotechnology. Suddenly, transnational corporations like DuPont, Monsanto, Novartis, and Syngenta, which have already caused so much misery, are casting themselves as do-gooders. Monsanto gave us Agent Orange, yet it is presented by the U.S. government and the corporate media as a good corporate citizen, concerned for the poor and hungry in the Third World. The U.S. government is "combating hunger" by allocating money from development-assistance programs to promote biotechnology in the Third World. And the civic groups that are opposing the corporate takeover of our food system and challenging genetic engineering—because we do not know its environmental and health consequences—are portrayed as selfish people who want to deny the Third World the benefits of biotechnology.

For years, oil companies have used "greenwashing" as a public-relations strategy, professing environmental concern to cover up their environmentally destructive activities. The biotech corporations are now using "poorwashing:" faking concern for the burgeoning, hungry population of the developing world while exploiting those populations in order to reap greater profits.

DJ: Let's talk about the debt the Third World owes to the World Bank and industrialized nations. U.S. foreign policy critic Noam Chomsky says, in essence, that the debt should be repaid, but it should be repaid by the people who actually received the loans, by which he means U.S.-imposed dictators, who siphoned off billions to their private bank accounts. But it should not be repaid by the citizens of the countries, who never got any of the money in the first place.

AM: But when the so-called aid has been given for, say, a large dam, who actually ends up with the money? It isn't a dictator, but the German, French, or American corporation that built the dam. Its investors are the ones who get paid. And the people of the nation got a dam they neither want nor need.

I've been involved in this struggle for a very long time. So much of it revolves around the notion of debt relief, which is just another version of the white man's burden. These backward people, the argument goes, just can't seem to figure out how to run their countries or their economies, and we need to keep perpetually giving them food and money.

But I'm not interested in debt relief. I'm interested in reparations. The Third World does not owe anyone anything. In fact, the industrialized nations owe us money.

DJ: How so?

AM: Take the case of my country, India—although any other country would provide just as good an example. Why did Columbus try to find a new route to India? Because it was a land of spices and wealth and gold, a country of grandeur. But when the Europeans came in—the East India Company, to be precise, which soon turned into the governing body for India and its people—my country saw the end of a golden age and the beginning of more than a hundred years of exploitation by the British. By the time India gained independence in 1947, this ancient civilization had become, at best, a "developing" country. There were many famines in India under British rule, during which millions died. And all the while, British India was being forced to export coffee, tea, rice, and wheat.

DJ: Just like today.

AM: And famines and starvation continue. After India gained independence, the Western powers once again found a way to colonize the country, first through the World Bank, and now through what I call the "unholy trinity" of the World Bank, the International Monetary Fund, and the World Trade Organization.

Third World countries were—and are—given bad loans, loans the people did not and do not want, loans about which we have never been consulted, loans for projects, such as large dams, that we protested and continue to protest. Loans for unpopular projects have been made to U.S.-backed dictators in the Philippines, Indonesia, Uganda. The World Bank gave the Philippines a loan to build a nuclear reactor in an area prone to seismic activity.

DJ: Was Uganda's Idi Amin put in place by the United States?

AM: Look at it this way: Uganda incurred most of its debt during Amin's regime. Do you think if the U.S. disapproved, the World Bank would have given him those loans? And although the loans were made to a brutal dictator, the people have been forced to pay them back, thus continuing the repression Amin started.

In country after country, the money has been funneled through the puppet governments and returned to the Western transnationals, all on the bent backs of the poor. Meanwhile, the poor nations have been compelled to slash their health and education programs, privatize the service sector, and cut down on jobs traditionally filled by women. Nurses, primary teachers: who needs them? Get rid of them.

And why do we have to do this? Because we have to service a debt that did not make a damn bit of difference in the day-to-day lives of ordinary people, working-class people, middle-class people. If you calculate how much money was given as a loan and how much has flowed back out, you'll understand why I say that the colonization has continued. The extraction of resources from these countries has, if anything, increased. The flow is always toward the rich, industrialized nations. We have not only repaid the loans made to corrupt regimes, we have overpaid them. And that overpayment did not start in the 1950s. This extraction has gone on for centuries, through various forms of colonization. It's time to give people in the Third World their fair due. It's time for reparations now.

The philosophy behind demanding reparations is that it says we are no longer victims, but people demanding our basic human rights, which have been violated for too long. And it's about accountability. Increasingly, we are beginning to hear about accountability for Third World leaders, such as Chilean dictator Augusto Pinochet, who was almost put on trial in Spain. It's time for that sort of accountability to be brought to the Western governments for what they have done to other cultures—and to their own people. It is time to try the Kissingers and McNamaras of the U.S.

DJ: Years ago, I asked a Tupac Amaru rebel what his group wanted for the people of Peru. His answer has haunted me ever since: "We want to be able to grow and distribute our own food. We already know how to do that. We merely need to be allowed to do so." In three sentences, he cut to the heart of colonialism, the heart of the problem we face.

AM: I couldn't agree more. Food is both personal and political. Food unites families and communities; across cultures, festivals based around harvest seasons are about sharing and strengthening communities. And food is political: the French Revolution wasn't driven just by the ideals of liberty, freedom, and egalitarianism. It was driven by the fact that there wasn't enough bread in Paris.

DJ: They could always eat cake.

AM: Or today, tulips.

Over the last three decades we have seen protests, rebellions, uprisings, and revolutions against this new colonialism, and these movements have often been centered around food. In the seventies, there were riots in Peru because the World Bank stipulated an increase in the price of bread. In the 1990s, the Zapatista uprising and the protests in Bolivia were spurred by food unavailability and privatization of the basic necessities of life. The same has been true in Pakistan and India. In 1995, villagers in Mexico stopped trains to loot them—not for gold, but for corn.

When we look at the growing discontent around the world, we find that many rebels have the same demand: the basic human right to be able to feed oneself. This is what the landless people's movement in Brazil wants, and the Poor People's Assembly in Thailand, and José Bové—the French farmer who drove his tractor through a McDonald's—and the farmers in India who burned the Cargill building and Monsanto's trial fields, and the small farmers in the U.S. These groups don't want power or wealth. They only want to be able to feed themselves and their families, and to live with dignity.

DJ: Why is it so central to Western civilization—and, more recently, to capitalism—to colonize and dispossess other peoples?

AM: I, too, wonder about this all the time. Is it intentional? Is it human nature to colonize and wreak havoc upon the poor? One thing I do know: when the rich are getting richer and the poor are getting poorer, these two things do not happen in a vacuum. The rich get richer at the expense of the poor. This mechanism is built into the capitalist system, around which our societies and our economies are organized. You know capitalism's "golden rule": whoever has the gold makes the rules. This system rewards greed and a complete lack of accountability on the part of CEOs, investors, and transnational corporations.

This is not a result of human nature. Nor is it something that just happens. It is a matter of power being exercised without any social, political, or environmental concerns. It is the planned exploitation of the poor on the part of those who stand to profit from it. And it is deeply ingrained in our society, because the powerful have built an entire economic and governmental structure to support it.

DJ: It seems pretty clear that access to land is central to everything we're talking about. Deny people that access, and you deny them self-sufficiency. Deny them self-sufficiency, and you can force them to work in your factories.

AM: The elites make a big mistake when they dispossess the working poor. They seem to believe that further dispossession will kill the poor people's spirit. But dispossessed people are angry people. Think about the courage of the poor who continue to occupy the land that the rich have stolen from them, even in the face of severe repression by private armies and police forces and death squads. We call them the "landless," but they are the ones who have earth in the cracks of their heels and under their fingernails. Their smell is of the land, and their blood washes the land for which they are killed. Look at them and tell me who has a right to the land.

What sustains these communities in the face of repression is the fact that they have nothing more to lose. When you have been beaten, tortured, and have seen your loved ones killed, there's only one thing to do: fight back.

DJ: It seems the capitalists might do better to follow the Roman poet Juvenal's advice, and give the masses "bread and circuses." Handouts cost less than repression. I remember reading years ago that the U.S. spent fifty thousand dollars for every Vietnamese person killed in that war. It occurred to me, even when I was a kid, that it would have been much cheaper—not to mention more humane—just to hand the Vietnamese a tenth of that money and say, "Be our friends." A lot of this repression is not only cruel but stupid.

AM: Perhaps if leaders were to do as you say and make sure people have roofs over their heads and food on their tables and healthcare and opportunities for education, then we would have more peace in our communities. But today's social and political structures are built on the foundation of centuries-old exploitation. The greed for more and more led the powerful to take a different path a long time ago. The exploitation has been going on for so long that the benevolence of dictators is no longer welcome.

I think we just plain missed the boat. We have an economic system based on greed, theft, lack of accountability, exploitation, colonization, racism, homophobia, sexism. This system has done severe damage to the soul of our society. I know it sounds like a cliché, but revolution is the answer. And this revolution will take a thousand shapes, from the Zapatista uprising to the thousands who challenged the G-8 Summit in Genoa, Italy. It's all revolution. Revolution takes place not only on the outside, but also in our hearts and minds, where it changes how we lead our day-to-day lives.

Activists must also deal with powerful interests within their own countries. The farmers' movement in India not only challenges obvious agents of colonialism—Monsanto, Cargill, and the rest—but the whole of Indian society, especially the middle class and the elites. The struggles in the Philippines not only are against the Americans, but are also struggles between Filipinos. The larger struggle is not merely between the impoverished nations of the South and the wealthy, industrialized North, because there's a South that lives in the North, and vice versa. There are 44 million Americans who have no healthcare. One in five American children is growing up in poverty. Similarly, there are elites in India who have much more in common with Bill Gates than you and I ever will.

DJ: A few years ago, a family farmer said to me, "Cargill gives me two choices: either I can cut my own throat, or they'll do it for me." The same could be said by farmers in any number of countries.

AM: In the south of India, you can go to village after village and not find a farmer who has both kidneys: they've all sold a kidney to feed their family. And there have been reports of farmers taking their own lives by consuming the same pesticides, the same poisons, they were told to use on their fields. They use this "gift" of industrial agriculture, which has cost them so much money and so much hope already, to end their own life.

In the U.S., farmers are killing themselves and trying to make it look like an accident so their families can get life insurance money. Forced out of their profession and unable to make a livelihood, they see no other way out.

At the World Food Summit in 1996, Dan Glickman, then the head of the United States Department of Agriculture (USDA), claimed that U.S. farmers would feed the world. He did not tell the summit that in the last few census polls, the category of "farmer" as a profession has been removed. According to the U.S. Census Bureau, farmers are not endangered; they're extinct. When Glickman talks about farmers, he really means corporations such as Cargill and Archer Daniels Midland—self-styled "Supermarket to the World." (Or, as I call it, Super-mark-up to the World.) They aren't U.S. farmers. They're agribusinesses.

DJ: But aren't they the ones who brought us the Green Revolution, which improved agricultural yields and thus saved millions of lives?

AM: This is one of the big myths. When I mention that India has a grain surplus, people often say to me that the Green Revolution—which is based on the use of chemical fertilizers and pesticides—is responsible for that. But we need to examine this claim closely.

From 1970 to 1990, the two main decades of the Green Revolution, the total food available per person in the world rose by 11 percent. This much is true. At the same time, the estimated number of hungry people fell by more than 150 million. So you might think there's a correlation between the increase in food due to the Green Revolution and the decrease in hunger. But if you eliminate China from the analysis, the number of hungry people in the world actually increased by 60 million. And it was not population growth that made for more hungry people. Remember, the total food available per person increased everywhere. What created more hunger was the absence of land reform and living-wage jobs.

The remarkable change in China, where the number of hungry people was more than cut in half, was the result of broad-based land reforms, which improved living standards. This is the little-known truth about the Green Revolution. Yes, food production increased, but did it have an impact on hunger? No.

We also need to examine the environmental costs of the Green Revolution. Use of chemical pesticides and fertilizers has resulted in the loss of almost a quarter of the topsoil in the U.S., and farming communities around the world have been devastated by salinization, waterlogging, and pests that have developed resistance to pesticides. I believe that around half the crop pests in the U.S. have developed resistance, and they cause around $2 billion worth of damage each year.

The bottom line is that the Green Revolution did not decrease hunger. It increased environmental degradation and cost of production for farmers who now depend on pesticides and fertilizers. The Green Revolution sounded the death knell for family farmers, the environment, and communities worldwide.

DJ: And there is currently an attempt to start a second Green Revolution based around GMOs.

AM: The same companies that benefited from the Green Revolution are now promoting genetic engineering. They recognize that the seed is the most important link in the food chain. Whoever controls the seed controls the food system. With genetic engineering, they can now patent the seeds. DuPont bought Pioneer Hybrid, a major seed company, for $8.5 billion; Monsanto has spent more than $7 billion on seed companies. The chemical companies are attempting to control the food system more than ever before.

DJ: And one of the ways chemical companies are attempting to control seeds is through technologies like Terminator, right?

AM: Yes, Terminator seeds are those that have been genetically modified not to reproduce. Their plants are sterile and do not produce viable seeds, meaning that farmers who use them have to purchase more seeds the next year. So the millenniums-old tradition that more than a billion farmers depend on—saving seeds from their harvest to use for the next season—is suddenly denied to them. I've yet to figure out how the companies can even pretend that this could benefit farmers in the Third World. The fact that those in power can control nature to the degree that they dictate whether or not a seed is fertile is sheer arrogance. It is ethically, economically, socially, and politically wrong, and there's no way around it.

DJ: Isn't Terminator banned right now from commercial use?

AM: In the face of worldwide opposition, commercial use of Terminator has been banned while further research is done on it. Recently, the USDA licensed the Terminator technology to its seed industry partner, Delta and Pine Land (D&PL). As a result of joint research, the USDA and D&PL are co-owners of three patents on the controversial technology. Although many of the chemical company giants hold patents on Terminator technology, D&PL is the only company that has publicly declared its intention to sell Terminator seeds commercially. This technology has been universally condemned by civil society, banned by international agricultural research institutes, censured by UN bodies, and even shunned by Monsanto—yet the U.S. government has officially licensed it to one of the world's largest seed companies.

Genetic engineering has also produced the Traitor technology, in which special characteristics of the seed—such as resistance to pests, or drought resistance—can be turned on and off only by certain chemicals produced, of course, by the same company that owns the seed patent. Biotech promoters claim that this technology will assist the poor and the hungry, but I wonder how it will benefit anyone but the chemical companies themselves.

DJ: How could a farmer be compelled to use that seed? It certainly doesn't seem to be in his or her best interest.

AM: Farmers around the world have been seduced by the promise of increased production and lower costs. The corporate media machine has sold this idea to both the farmers and the policymakers. But many farmers have been denied any choice over whether to grow genetically modified crops. Some of them do it without even meaning to do so. Percy Schneider, a farmer in Canada, was served with a lawsuit by Monsanto because detectives hired by the company found evidence of their patented seed in his field. Now, how did it get there? He didn't plant it. Its presence was a result of genetic pollution from a neighboring field. Because some plants are pollinated by the wind and others by insects, they can't be entirely contained.

DJ: Honeybees have been known to fly a dozen miles.

AM: Say you want to be an organic farmer. If a neighbor, or even someone many miles away, uses genetically modified seeds, that crop can cross-pollinate with your own. And there are other concerns, as well. For example, organic farmers have long used Bacillus thuringiensis (Bt), a naturally occurring insect toxin, as a pesticide, but genetic engineers have spliced Bt into cotton, potato, and other plants. This overuse will quickly result in insects resistant to Bt, forcing organic farmers to hop on the bandwagon of using toxic chemicals.

DJ: How do we bring about this revolution that you're talking about?

AM: The revolution has already begun. We see it around us. It is multicultural and has the energy and passion of youth and the spirit of the working poor. Think about the protests at the World Trade Organization meeting in Seattle. The battle there was not between the industrialized nations of the North and the so-called developing nations of the South. The youth of the Northern nations were out in the streets—all those beautiful young faces—while the leaders of the Southern nations were walking out of the meetings, saying, "This is not good enough."

This revolution is built on cross-border organizing, forming links between local and global issues, and seeing the relationship between "structural adjustment programs" in the Third World and welfare reform—or just plain economics—in the U.S.

We need to nurture this revolution in our minds and souls. We need to sustain it with the determination that we will no longer ask whether we can speak. We are going to demand that our voices be heard. And we will sustain it with the knowledge that these are our fields, and the land is our inheritance.

This revolution recognizes access to food, water, health care, education— every basic necessity of life—as a human right, not a need. If it were only a need, it could be serviced by a corporation. As a human right, it cannot be sold by anyone. This revolution is not dependent on the benevolence of dictators but gains its legitimacy from its soldiers: the landless and the dispossessed. This revolution is nonviolent and based on the truth: that the land belongs to the landless, the farms to the small family farmers—who are the best stewards of the land—and our natural resources to the local communities. And this revolution does not differentiate between civil rights and economic, social, and cultural rights. It recognizes that land and liberty, jobs and justice go together. Freedom from want is as important as freedom from fear.

The success of this people's movement depends on us. I have one message for all: get involved. It does not have to be at a policy level in Washington, D.C. You do not have to change your lifestyle or quit your job. You might choose involvement in the community, such as the local housing association, or the food bank. You might call or write your Congressional Representative. But do get involved. Change starts at the local level. If power is not taken back there, nothing will change at the national or international level.

Each human being has an incredible amount of power that comes from having human rights. So let's educate ourselves about our rights: the right to unionize, the right to have a decent job, the right to feed our families. These rights are not dependent on the whims and fancies of corporations or presidents. They are dependent on real people exercising real democracy. And that requires that we get involved. Human rights are never won without a fight.

JULIET SCHOR

Interview conducted
on June 16, 2003,
by telephone.

"Imperial power," says Juliet Schor, with an engaging bluntness, "leads directly to ecological degradation." Schor has spent years writing about the global economic system with a clarity both necessary and rare— necessary because our planet is under assault, and human rights along with it; rare because corporations need the American public to remain mystified about the destruction inherent in corporate power and profits. Through the tightening noose of neoliberal policies, corporations have been able to force global wages to inconceivable lows: for example, seven cents an hour for workers in Chinese toy factories. The resulting drop in prices has led to the average American child now receiving sixty-nine toys a year. Multiply that broadly across markets in rich countries, and the level of consumption can only strip the planet bare. Schor's message is ultimately a call to action: "We have to organize against the system. The system is not going to disappear on its own."

Juliet Schor taught at Harvard University for seventeen years and is currently Professor of Sociology at Boston College. She is author of the national bestseller, *The Overworked American: The Unexpected Decline of Leisure* (Basic Books), and *The Overspent American: Why We Want What We Don't Need* (Harper Perennial). Schor's latest book is *Born to Buy: The Commercialized Child and the New Consumer Culture* (Scribner), which is both an account of marketing to children from inside marketing agencies and an assessment of how these activities are affecting children. Schor has served as a consultant to the United Nations, at the World Institute for Development Economics Research, and to the United Nations Development Program. In 1998 she received the George Orwell Award for Distinguished Contributions to Honesty and Clarity in Public Language from the National Council of Teachers of English.

Derrick Jensen: What is the relationship between globalization and empire, and both of these and environmental degradation?

Juliet Schor: The simplest formulation is that the current workings of the global economy are degrading the planet through their contribution to excessive consumerism, and American power makes that all possible.

DJ: How does that work?

JS: Central to globalization is a pressure to drive down prices. This in turn leads to increased consumption, which then leads to greater degradation.

DJ: Where does empire fit in?

JS: The short answer is that military and police power are crucial in repressing wages and costs around the world.

DJ: What is your definition of empire?

JS: In this specific case—American empire—I'm talking about a combination of economic, political, and military power, which allows the U.S. to assert its economic interests or point of view outside its own borders. So, for example, why did the U.S. invade Iraq? I would argue that this projection of political and military power has a strong economic motivation behind it. Similarly, you see the projection of political power in the Bretton Woods Institutions—the

WTO, the IMF, the World Bank—which are used to set the rules of global trade and investment so that they operate in the interests mostly of American corporations (and more generally of multinationals). Both military power and the Bretton Woods Institutions have been important in the weakening of labor and repression of wages.

DJ: How does this work?

JS: Let's talk about apparel, because I think it's a good example of the ways in which American power shapes the global economy and in turn leads to environmental degradation.

Apparel consumption dramatically increased in the United States over the 1990s, and in particular in the second half of the 1990s. It's still increasing. And that growth came through imports. In 1996 the United States imported 7.3 billion units of apparel, narrowly defined—meaning basically undergarments, pants, tops, dresses, and so on, as opposed to a wider range which would include accessories, hats, and so forth. In 2001, the last year for which I've been able to get data, the imports were 12.75 billion units. Domestic consumption increased 73 percent in five years (and of course it increased from 1991 to 1996 as well). That's phenomenal. I calculate that in 2001 the per capita consumption of new units of apparel will be about forty-five pieces. That's almost one per week. For women it's much higher: women consume about 40 percent more apparel than men, which means their annual consumption is in the mid-sixties. That's an extraordinary increase in a short period of time.

Throughout the 1990s you had high levels of what the industry calls "churning," or the discard of used items. So Goodwill, for example, the major institution which acquires used items, saw its rates of intake go up by ten percent per year over the decade. By the end of the decade they were only able to place between five and fifteen percent of what they took into their stores. That's how huge the discard volume had become. The wholesale market for clothing collapsed until the per pound price of clothing dropped to about two or three cents a pound, i.e., virtually nothing, virtually free goods.

Historically, clothing was a highly priced commodity, rather valuable, with people holding relatively small inventories, and also for the most part using it up either within households or communities. Clothes would cascade down a series of uses from special occasion to everyday usage to eventually being used for rags and then disintegrating. That process happened across households too, sometimes, as people traded.

Now you're in a situation in which used clothing has become cheaper than rice or beans. It's hard to even give it away: no one will pay for it. In this country we're drowning in a sea of clothing. The key to this transformation has to do with the prices, because the last decade saw a decline in apparel prices. In particular at the end of the 1990s you get a very sharp decline, brought on by the Asian financial crisis.

DJ: I don't understand.

JS: On the other side of the ocean, at the point of production, apparel wages have become abysmally low. Take Bangladesh, which by the end of the decade had become the fourth largest apparel exporter to the United States, rising from nothing in a very short time. Wages there start at seven to eight cents per hour at the bottom of the scale, maxing out at seventeen to eighteen cents an hour.

DJ: We hear all the time though that that's good for people in the Third World because otherwise they would simply starve to death.

JS: It's far more complicated than that. Now, it certainly is true that once you have a lot of global activity by multinational corporations which disrupt domestic agriculture and industry and displace people, once people no longer have a means of livelihood, giving them employment can sometimes be better than not giving them employment. But even once they've been dispossessed, they're much better off with higher wages than lower wages.

DJ: The key seems to be that once you've deprived them of the possibility of raising their own food by depriving them of access to their own land you've got them at a place where you can pay them seven cents an hour.

JS: Yes. And the important point about the Asian financial crisis is that it's an example of how the global economy—mostly operating with trends in the financial markets—led to these very low wages. Speculative attacks on the currencies of a group of Asian countries in the late 1990s—1997 to 1998—led to enormous dislocation, a dramatic growth in unemployment, and economic collapse, all of which yielded declines in income. So for example, in a place like Indonesia, from pre-crisis 1995 to post-crisis 2001, per capita income declined 29 percent. In Malaysia, it was 17 percent. In Thailand, 19.5 percent. These are monumental erosions in standards of living. Not surprisingly, that then leads to declining wages in the garment industry, not just in those countries, but in all the other countries which are now competing in a global market for the sourcing of apparel. That's why the Asian financial crisis affects Bangladeshi wages, and Chinese wages, which are also below twenty-five cents an hour.

DJ: Does it also affect U.S. wages?

JS: Probably not much. The U.S. apparel industry is fairly well insulated. Foreign manufacturers apply a little bit of pressure, but for the most part they're making different things: a lot of the low wage mass production apparel already fled this country.

DJ: Wait. Americans can buy T-shirts for so cheap they're almost free. Isn't that good news for American consumers?

JS: Well, it's good news for American consumers if you think more T-shirts and higher inventories of apparels sitting in our closets contribute to people's well-being.

DJ: Isn't that perception commonly accepted, especially within mainstream economics?

JS: It is the conventional view, but there is increasing evidence to show it is misguided, for a couple of reasons. The first is that you have to look on the other side of the costs of production. What about the environmental impacts not being taken into account in the price? They haven't been internalized. So, whenever you have a market externality like that, the idea that more stuff makes you better off doesn't follow, because, for example, it might be befouling your air or your water or your environment, which in this case it is. And to figure out what the ultimate welfare impact is going to be you're going to have to take that into account. But right now we're not taking that into account, because nobody's paying for that pollution.

DJ: People are certainly paying with their lives.

JS: Factory owners and shareholders aren't forced to prevent it or clean it up. Which means that the price is too low.

DJ: But from the perspective especially of American economists, who cares? So what if the air becomes befouled in Bangladesh?

JS: That's not exactly fair to economists, in the sense that the theory doesn't say you shouldn't take account of pollution. The theory would say, I suppose— but I'm not sure this is even true—that the people in Bangladesh would prefer income to a pollution-free environment.

There's another point I want to make, though, about people's well-being. The idea that the well-being of an American is unaffected by exploiting people in other places is wrongheaded. Certainly if you ask American consumers if they care whether their goods are made under sweatshop conditions they will say *yes*, they do care. They'd rather pay more. But right now there's virtually no structural mechanism in place to allow those preferences to be realized in the market. In fact just the opposite is true, which is that—and this is the point where I started—American power is being used to repress wages. This happens directly, through support of corrupt regimes that use direct force to repress workers' attempts to organize—that is, where the people who own the factories are often the people who run the government and also indirectly through the operation of the Bretton Woods institutions and the global economy.

There is yet another point to be made about this, which has to do with the relationship between consumption and well-being. It turns out that the evidence fairly consistently shows that once you get beyond poverty, increases in consumption don't do much to increase people's subjective well-being. So, for example, there have been big increases in income per head in places like Japan, Europe, and the United States since World War II, yet subjective well-being hasn't increased in these places over that time. More and more evidence shows that the relationship between consumption and well-being operates mainly through relative comparisons. I'm better off—I have a higher subjective well-being—when I move up the hierarchy in my own society, my own reference group. This is because people are very social in the way they experience consumption. If they improve their income relative to their reference group, their well-being goes up, but if everybody's standard of living goes up at the same time, so everybody gets a cashmere sweater and a silk blouse and five other new items, nobody feels better off.

DJ: In a sense it would only increase my subjective sense of well-being to have cheap clothing if I were the only person who had access to it.

JS: Right. That would mean you get a higher real income.

I want to go back to the environmental impacts of clothing production. People often think of it as a clean commodity, but it isn't. Very high levels of pesticides are used to produce cottons—for use in T-shirts, for example—which pollute water supplies and soil. This has a huge impact in the United States, where run-off from cotton cultivation has polluted water supplies in lots of states.

DJ: And there's a huge drawdown of aquifers in, for example, Arizona, where for some stupid reason they're trying to grow cotton.

JS: Cotton is a very resource-intensive crop. It uses lots of water and is also very hard on the soil.

Another impact of the apparel industry is the heavy use of toxic chemicals in synthetic dyes. This has health impacts both on workers in garment factories and also on consumers. There have been studies in Europe showing very high levels of allergic and toxic reactions by both kids and adults to the dyes in clothing. Germany, for example, has banned ago-dyes, which are the most common type of textile dyes, and which Americans know nothing about. Even though the entire European Union is contemplating an ago-dye ban, that's not even on the agenda here.

Other examples of impacts include overgrazing by goatherds in Mongolia because of the rage for cheap cashmere sweaters, which has led to price declines and then more herds, more overgrazing, and more ecosystem disruption; deforestation for the production of tencel, which is a wood-based fabric; and use of toxics and petroleum for synthetics, which globally comprise a major portion of textiles.

With the exception of hemp, which is a small but growing and very favored crop by ecologists, virtually every textile source has big environmental impacts.

And you've got to put those on the other side of the ledger when you're thinking about well-being.

Although apparel is, as I said, a canonical example, you can see similar developments in lots of other commodities, where you have repression of wages abroad, declining prices for U.S. consumers, and increasing quantities consumed, whether you're talking about consumer electronics, other types of near apparel items, whatever.

Toys make another interesting case. The average American child now consumes sixty-nine new toys a year. Americans spend $29.4 billion per year on toys. The majority of those toys now come from China, where you see again extremely exploitative working conditions, with wages ranging again from about seven cents an hour at the bottom to about thirty-three at the top. Here in the States, toy prices have fallen by a third in the last ten years. This dramatic decline has led to a huge increase in volume, until it's now 3.6 billion units of toys a year.

This is true in commodity after commodity. If you look at the index of department store prices over the last ten years, what you find is that overall, department store prices have fallen by a third. That's phenomenal. And in durable goods, which have high levels of imports, the decline was 57 percent.

DJ: I don't mean to be a jerk, but doesn't that mean the global economy is working?

JS: It means the pressures to reduce wages and costs abroad are considerable enough that it has changed how economies operate. Japan and Korea would be examples of how economies used to operate. The investment comes in, the nation produces for export, and wages rise over time. Workers become more productive, more powerful. Workers in Korea and Japan experienced extraordinary increases in their standards of living. The wages of workers in manufacturing rose.

But now, the reverse happens. Because of the restructuring of the global economy along neoliberal policy lines, because of the global sweatshop and the hypermobility of capital, whenever a labor market starts to move in the direction of workers being able to capture a bit more of the value of their own production, capital flees, goes to another country where people are even more exploited, more disorganized. So, for example, several corporations—Nike is a famous example—pulled out of South Korea as soon as those workers started to ask for better working conditions and higher wages. The corporations moved to Indonesia. When the same thing happened there they moved to Vietnam. And they move to Bangladesh, they move to China. And so on.

In the United States workers get something like 60 to 65 percent of the value of the products they produce. That's the share that goes to wages. On the other hand, there are estimates showing that Nike workers receive half a percent of the value of the product. These workers are receiving the lowest levels of labor share recorded.

You asked whether workers are better off with these jobs than with no jobs at all. There was a time when I think it could be said that workers' lives improved with an influx of investment and jobs. But right now people are being drawn into a global economy that operates in such a way that it's virtually impossible for them to gain even a subsistence level of income through their participation.

DJ: I'm thinking about Robert Jay Litton's book *The Nazi Doctors*. He made the point that many of the doctors who worked at Auschwitz did what was in the best interests of the Jews, with one crucial caveat: they stayed strictly within the framing conditions of the Auschwitz mindset. Within the context of confining Jews, starving them, working them to death, and assembly-line mass murder, the doctors did the best they could. Stepping outside those framing conditions, of course, they actively participated in genocide.

I think we can say the same thing here: so long as the people are allowed to stay within these neoliberal framing conditions where people do not have autonomy, democracy, or access to land, they will be given these choices: they can either starve to death, or they can get this crappy job . . .

JS: . . . and starve to death.

It's a really important point, because what's happened is that the political shifts, and the shifts in the structure of the global economy, have basically yielded two horribly unpalatable alternatives.

Right now the no-win debate seems to be framed between one side that says that these people are exploited, and another—the supporters of the global economy—who says, "Well, they're better off than if we weren't exploiting them." It's like the famous Joan Robinson quote, "The only thing worse than being exploited by a capitalist is not being exploited by a capitalist." But that's no longer an accurate description of what happens in the global economy. I think the question we have to come back with is not, "Are they better off than without a job?" which is what Nike and the other companies continually force us to only ask, but "Can we pay them higher wages?" The answer to that of course is yes, there's no doubt about it.

DJ: Or how about not asking but demanding that people have access to their own land, and thus their own self-sufficiency? The problem is, why should Nike or the U.S. government go along with any of this?

JS: We try to get them to do that through political pressure, consumer pressure, through building a movement of people who are saying, "Enough already! The global economy is unethical, it's wrong. It's destroying the environment, which means among other things it's shortsighted. And we are morally and pragmatically opposed to it."

DJ: Given the whole sordid history of civilization, and more specifically empire, why should those in power care? How do we make those in power care? Because they're obviously making the rules that cause this. They'll never say, "Oh my god, this was all an accident, how could this possibly have happened? Let's fix it." This enslavement of the poor is precisely what they have set out to do.

JS: Of course there is no simple answer. People have to organize and put on the pressure in lots of different ways. I think so far as the consumer goods issue goes, we need to remember that these companies are very sensitive to public image. The brand value—the very thing that makes them able to charge a hundred dollars for a shoe that only cost them a couple of dollars to make—is easily destroyed. That's one point. And activists have had some success in targeting brands, forcing these companies to respond. Unfortunately, activists have so far been for the most part outmaneuvered by the companies, who have responded in ways that basically amount to public relations tactics and not substantive change. We'll see whether that continues over the next five to ten years.

As the system becomes more and more dysfunctional in various ways—for example, as the ecological unsustainability increases and the costs start to rebound back onto the system—the system's contradictions will become more difficult to ignore. One of these contradictions is the fact that people don't have the income to buy products. Another is that in a world in which you have growing inequalities, the cost of maintaining those inequalities gets higher. People revolt, and those in power need more police and military to keep them down. These factors will all play a role in transforming society. All of the contradictions allow you to split the people in power, so eventually you get one group that starts to see the world differently, seeing that we need a structural change, we need a paradigm change. That's what you hope for. And you organize the people who are directly being hurt.

The more dysfunctional the system gets, the easier it is to split the elites, and the easier it is to mobilize people being hurt by the elites.

DJ: I want to go back to this whole consumer question for a second. If increased consumption does not lead to increased well-being once you get beyond the point of having food, clothing, and shelter, why then does this consumption continue to explode? Why the increase in apparel usage? Why the increase in toys? If it doesn't make us happier, why do we do it?

JS: I think the first answer to that is that we perceive ourselves as being locked into a system in which consumption has a very high social valence, and in which our forms of social competition are to a large extent organized around consumption and income. That's what is socially valued. Although participating in the system may not make you better off, if you hold onto the mindset and the values of that system, to fall behind makes you very much worse off. Unless of course you decide to opt out of the dominant system of social meaning and value altogether.

Unfortunately there's been a rapid escalation of consumption norms in the United States in roughly the last fifteen years, which means that people feel increasing pressure to keep up with those norms. The vast majority of people's income and wealth isn't increasing as fast as are those norms. So it puts them under a lot of pressure to work longer hours, take on more debt, and so on. That escalation has a big cost. But if there's just one game in town, you've got to play it.

Now of course we see groups of people saying, "Enough already, I want to opt out of that and create a new system of social meaning." I talk about them as downshifters, voluntary simplifiers, and so forth, people who reject the dominant meaning system. But there's a lot in place to keep us tied into that dominant system. There's the cultural/social side that I've been talking about, and there's also the economic side, which is that people are terrified about the idea of the economy collapsing, and about losing their access to income, so they see no alternative to a consumer-driven growth-oriented economy. That's all been drummed into their heads pretty seriously. And there's a political stranglehold in which you have a bipartisan consensus around growth and consumerism. There's not even a space in the dominant political discourse for people to raise questions about it. Jimmy Carter did it and got absolutely slammed for it.

DJ: Can we talk about non-manufactured commodities?

JS: The relationship between empire and agricultural and energy commodities is a little bit different than for manufactured goods, because with manufactured goods the story is mostly about repressing wages. In the so-called commodities cases it's about manipulating the market for commodities because you're not paying wages to the producers, whether they're farmers, natural resource extractors, or whatever.

But it all boils down to the same thing, which is imperial power being used to exploit the poor. In the case of commodities it's through the depression of prices. Here I think the canonical example is what we in graduate school were taught to call the example of the cheap banana. Bananas are an exotic and expensive tropical import. They should be very highly priced. But in the 1950s and 1960s the banana became incredibly cheap in the United States, like apples or potatoes, which are low cost domestic produce available on a year-round basis, and a staple of daily life. How did bananas move into that category? The answer is that U.S. companies, United Fruit in particular, established plantation agriculture in places like Central America, with Guatemala being the famous example. The company also took over other key parts of the Guatemalan economy—railroads, ports, electricity, etc.—developing a monopoly position in that economy. Then when the first democratically elected Guatemalan president, Jacob Arbenz, said, "We want to give Guatemala back to the Guatemalans," United Fruit arranged a CIA coup, complete with aerial bombardment, to overthrow Arbenz. This ushered in decades of terror and death. In this famous case, more than a hundred thousand people were murdered by a right-wing government put in after the CIA coup. What you see here is a direct linkage between American imperial power and these cheap commodities, because imperial power created the structural conditions necessary for very low wages, plantation agriculture, and cheap bananas.

If you look at what's happened in the period of the neoliberal global economy, which is basically 1980 to the present, primary commodities prices—let's exclude energy for the moment—have declined. Through the 1980s they declined about

45 percent, and then there was a stabilization for about five years. But since the mid-1990s there has been a decline of an additional twenty percent. That's more than a 50 percent decline. In some cases even more spectacular collapses in prices—for example in coffee and cocoa, products that have absolutely impoverished producers—have wiped out huge numbers of cultivators. These stories are very similar to the story of bananas, which is that by altering the structural conditions of the economy, taking control of those markets, the imperial countries have been able to engineer terms of trade that are very much in their favor and that allow them to import huge quantities of very cheap products.

All of these activities have immense ecological impacts, especially when family or community farms give way to intensive highly chemical industrial agriculture that is an inevitable response to these framing conditions. Imperial power leads directly to ecological degradation and unsustainable food systems.

DJ: What about oil?

JS: As we all know, over a very long period, the use of military power to exert control over foreign oil supplies has been central to U.S. policy. This has been especially true since the 1970s.

DJ: Which, not coincidentally, is when U.S. oil production peaked. Since that time it's been dropping.

JS: I believe that 9/11 marked a watershed moment in terms of U.S. military and foreign policy thinking on oil because it awakened American strategic thinkers—the people who control foreign policy and the military—to a reality they hadn't seen before, which was the extreme precariousness of their control of Saudi oil. Because the Saudi regime was increasingly unstable—after all, it was Saudis who bombed the World Trade Center—the U.S. strategic planners figured they had to secure access to another major source of oil.

So what did those who run the United States do? First, they invaded Afghanistan. A key reason for that invasion was to open up the Central Asian pipeline. They'd been trying to do that for quite a while. And after that? They increased in a big way their military presence in central Asia.

If you look at the president's energy plan, you find it's a pretty stunning document. It predicts a 33 percent increase in U.S. oil consumption in the next seventeen years, along with of course a major decline in domestic production. They predict a 19 million barrel daily shortfall by the year 2020. And if Saudi Arabia is unavailable, Iraq is the only other place.

U.S. policymakers gain another advantage by achieving political control over Iraqi oil: they are then able to have a much bigger impact on oil's price. Dropping the price of oil is a wealth transfer from Iraqis and other oil producers to American consumers, just as happened with the coup in Guatemala. Consumers around the world will benefit from decreases in price, but this is especially important to the U.S. economy because it has such an inefficient use of fossil fuels. Any drop in the price of oil gives American businesses an edge against competitors.

DJ: Once again, if those in power are going to invade over bananas, and certainly invade over oil, what do we do?

JS: Certainly the United States has a long and sordid history of military intervention to secure access to raw materials and bondholders' interests. This is a longstanding problem.

DJ: It's not just Bush's fault.

JS: Nor is it just bananas and oil, although oil is crucial.

The short answer is that we have to organize against the system. There's no alternative to that. The system is not going to disappear on its own. And it's not an easy task. But there are a couple of ways we can make our organizing more effective.

In response to the buildup to the invasion of Iraq we saw an extraordinary coming together of a global movement, in this case a global peace movement. I think this lays the foundation for a global justice and peace and ecological movement. Those are the three key factors I think this movement needs to bring together. And that's what I try to do with my analysis: show how anti-war concerns really are very closely aligned—because of the structural operation of the industrial capitalist system—with global justice and ecological concerns.

A key dimension to success for that movement will be its ability to articulate an alternative. A big part of why globalization has been able to proceed as rapidly as it has, and with as ineffective opposition, is that it has positioned itself as inevitable. Those in power have talked us into believing the global economy is natural: they've made it feel as inevitable and uncontrollable as the weather. That is very powerful for people. It is something activists can and must directly speak to. The more we begin to actualize on the ground alternatives on a small and local scale, and the more we articulate alternatives in terms of our intellectual work, the better chance we have of stopping this atrocity-inducing system.

DJ: What are the alternatives?

JS: There's a wide range of alternative economic arrangements involving relocalization. We see that with food, for example, as people increasingly tie into local food systems and local food networks. Then you have local businesses creating local currencies which draw in local consumers. You have consumer movements directly addressing issues of exploitation and sweatshops. You have cooperatives—democratic economic forms—which give the people actually involved in the economic activity more control over what they're doing, which give communities more control over their economies, and which relocalize as much as possible. All of these function as alternatives to the multinational globalized economy, because that's based on a model of extreme centralization of power, extreme centralization of wealth and ownership.

RAMSEY CLARK

Interview conducted on
November 20, 2000, at
his office in New York City.

W hen I picture a high-ranking government official, I think of someone who is corrupt. I think of a corporate shill. I think of someone who is not a friend to the people of this country. I think of Lord Acton's famous line about power corrupting, and absolute power corrupting absolutely. I think of the disdain with which so many Americans have viewed so many of their leaders for so many years.

Former attorney general Ramsey Clark is different. Despite having once been the chief law enforcement officer of this country, he consistently takes the side of the oppressed.

Born to power—Clark's father was attorney general in the 1940s and later a Supreme Court justice—the University of Chicago Law School graduate was appointed Assistant Attorney General by John F. Kennedy in 1961 and went on to head that department as Attorney General under Lyndon Johnson from 1967 to 1969. During his years in the Justice Department, Clark was a staunch supporter of the Civil Rights Movement. While in charge of government efforts to protect the protesters in Alabama, he witnessed firsthand "the enormous violence that was latent in our society toward unpopular people." He had a similar experience when he was sent to Los Angeles after the rioting in Watts and discovered abuses by the police and the National Guard.

Back then Clark didn't take the strong antiwar stance he advocates today, but his Justice Department record boasts some major accomplishments: he supervised the drafting and passage of the Voting Rights Act of 1965 and the Civil Rights Act of 1968. He denounced police shootings and authorized prosecution of police on charges of brutality and wrongful death. He opposed electronic surveillance and refused to authorize an FBI wiretap on Martin Luther King, Jr. He fought hard against the death penalty and won, putting a stay on federal executions that lasted until 2001, when Timothy McVeigh's death sentence was carried out.

After a failed bid for the Senate in 1976, Clark abandoned government service and set out to provide legal defense to victims of oppression. As an attorney in private practice, he has represented many controversial clients over the years, among them antiwar activist Father Philip Berrigan; Native American political prisoner Leonard Peltier; the Branch Davidians, whose compound in Waco, Texas, was destroyed by government agents; Sheik Omar Abdel-Rahman, who was accused of masterminding the World Trade Center bombing; and Lori Berenson, an American held in a Peruvian prison for allegedly supporting the revolutionary Tupac Amaru movement there. Clark's dedication to defending unpopular, and even hated, figures has also led him to represent such clients as Bosnian Serb leader Radovan Karadzic and far-right extremist Lyndon LaRouche.

Clark is founder and chairperson of the International Action Center, the largest antiwar movement in the United States. A vocal critic of U.S. military actions around the globe, he calls government officials "international outlaws," accusing them of "killing innocent people because we don't like their leader." He has traveled to Iraq, North Vietnam, Serbia, and other embattled regions of the world to investigate the effects of American bombing and economic sanctions there. The sanctions, he says, are particularly inhumane: "They're like the neutron bomb, which is the most 'inspired' of all weapons, because it kills the people and preserves the property, the wealth. So you get the wealth and you don't have the baggage of the hungry, clamoring poor."

After the Gulf War, in 1991, Clark initiated a war crimes tribunal, which tried and found guilty President George Bush, General Colin Powell, and General Norman Schwarzkopf, among others. Clark went on to write a book, *The Fire This Time* (Thunder's Mouth Press), describing the crimes he says were committed by U.S. and NATO forces during the Gulf War. When asked why he focuses on the crimes of his own country, instead of those committed by Iraq, Clark says that we, as citizens, need to announce our principles and "force our government to adhere to them. When you see your government violating those principles, you have the highest obligation to correct what your government does, not point the finger at someone else."

The interview took place on a dreary day in November 2000. But Clark's criticisms of U.S. foreign policy are, if anything, more relevant today. I met with Clark in the offices of the International Action Center. Books lined every wall, except for a fairly large area devoted to photographs of Clark's two children, his numerous grandchildren, and his wife of more than fifty years.

Derrick Jensen: According to the federal government's Defense Planning Guide of 1992, the first objective of U.S. foreign policy is to convince potential rivals that they "need not aspire" to "a more aggressive posture to defend their legitimate interests." The implication seems to be that the U.S. intends not to let other countries actively defend their own interests. To what extent does U.S. foreign policy in action reflect that goal?

Ramsey Clark: Our foreign policy has been a disaster since long before that planning guide—for a lot longer than we'd like to believe. We can look all the way back to the arrogance of the Monroe Doctrine, when the United States said, "This hemisphere is ours," ignoring all the other people who lived here, too. For a part of this past century, there were some constraints on our capacity for arbitrary military action—what you might call the inhibitions of the Cold War—but with the collapse of the Soviet Union, we've acquired a headier sense of what we can get away with.

Our overriding purpose, from the beginning right through to the present day, has been world domination—that is, to build and maintain the capacity to coerce everybody else on the planet—nonviolently, if possible; and violently, if necessary. But the purpose of our foreign policy of domination is not just to make the rest of the world jump through hoops; the purpose is to facilitate our exploitation of resources. And insofar as any people or states get in the way of our domination, they must be eliminated—or, at the very least, shown the error of their ways.

I'm not talking about just military domination. U.S. trade policies are driven by the exploitation of poor people the world over. The Vietnam War is a good example of the United States's military and economic inhumanity. We have punished Vietnam's government and people mercilessly, just because they want freedom. The Vietnamese people had to fight for thirty years to achieve freedom, first against the French, and then against the United States. I used to be criticized for saying that the Vietnamese suffered 2 million casualties, but I've noticed that people now say 3 million without much criticism. Yet that war was nothing compared to the effects of twenty years of sanctions, from 1975 to 1995, which brought the Vietnamese people—a people who had proven to be invincible when threatened by physical force on their own land—down to such dire poverty that they were taking to open boats in stormy seas, and drowning, to get to a refugee camp in Hong Kong, a place no one in his or her right mind would want to be. They went simply because they saw no future in their own country.

I went to North Vietnam in the summer of 1971, when the U.S. was trying to destroy civilian dikes through bombing. Our government figured that if it could destroy Vietnam's capacity for irrigation, it could starve the people into submission.

DJ: Which, in itself, is a war crime.

RC: Sure, but since when does international law stop the U.S. government—except when it comes to laws made by the World Trade Organization, where it's to the advantage of the owners of capital for the government to obey them?

The U.S. figured that if the Vietnamese couldn't control their water supply, then they couldn't grow rice, and they wouldn't be able to feed themselves. At that time, they were producing about five tons of rice to the hectare, which is extremely productive. The economy was based on the women. The men were living in tunnels to the south with a bag of rice, a bag of ammunition, and a rifle; some had been there for years. And we were still bombing them mercilessly, inflicting heavy casualties. Yet they survived.

The sanctions, on the other hand, brought their economy down below that of Mozambique—then the poorest country in the world, with a per capita income of about eighty dollars per year.

All of this reflects a U.S. foreign policy that is completely materialistic and enforced by violence, or the threat of violence, and economic coercion.

DJ: Do you think most Americans would agree that U.S. foreign policy has been "a disaster"?

RC: Sadly, I think most Americans don't have an opinion about our foreign policy. Worse than that, when they do think about it, it's in terms of the demonization of enemies and the exaltation of our capacity for violence.

When the Gulf War started in 1991, you could almost feel a reverence come over the country. We had a forty-two-day running commercial for militarism. Nearly everybody was glued to CNN, and whenever they saw a Tomahawk cruise missile taking off from a navy vessel somewhere in the Persian Gulf, they practically stood up and shouted, "Hooray for America!" But that missile was going to hit a market in Basra or someplace, destroy three hundred food stalls, and kill forty-two very poor people. And we considered that a good thing.

It's very difficult to debate military spending in this country today. This is unbelievable, because our military spending is absolutely, certifiably insane. Just to provide one example: we still have twenty-two commissioned Trident nuclear submarines, which are first-strike weapons. Any one of those submarines can launch twenty-four missiles simultaneously. Each of those missiles can contain as many as seventeen independently targeted, maneuverable nuclear warheads. And each of those warheads can travel seven thousand nautical miles and supposedly hit within three hundred feet of its predetermined target. If we fire them in opposite directions, we can span fourteen thousand nautical miles: halfway around the world at the equator. This means we can take out 408 centers of human population, hitting each with a nuclear warhead ten times as powerful as the bomb that incinerated Nagasaki.

DJ: This is all from one submarine?

RC: One submarine. And we have twenty-two of them. It's an unthinkable machine. Why would you have it? What kind of mind would conceive of such a machine? What justification could there be for its existence? What would be the meaning of daring to use it?

Yet the debate about military spending in this country never raises these questions. Think back to 1980, when President Carter and Governor Reagan were arguing about the military budget. At that time, you could see the end of the Cold War approaching; the risk of superpower conflict was waning rapidly. Carter came in with a 7 percent increase in the budget, when it should have been reduced. And Reagan, of course, topped him with a proposal for an 11 percent increase. Carter's response was that he could spend 7 percent more effectively than Reagan could spend 11 percent, so we'd be stronger on Carter's program. Nowhere in this debate did we—or do we now—hear anything about the morality or the sanity (even the fiscal sanity) of such huge military budgets.

Our foreign policy is based on the use of our military might as an enforcer, exactly as Teddy Roosevelt implied when he said that we should "speak softly and carry a big stick." What does that mean? It means: "Do what I say, or I'll smash your head in. I won't make a lot of noise about it; I'll just do it."

DJ: How many times has the United States invaded Latin America in the last two hundred years?

RC: It depends on who's doing the counting, but in the twentieth century alone, it was undoubtedly almost once per year. Off the top of my head, I could count probably seventy instances.

DJ: And, of course, it was the same in the nineteenth century.

RC: We sent the word out pretty early. We had to worry about the British and the Spanish for a long time, but we were determined to make this "our" hemisphere—though we certainly didn't confine ourselves to just this side of the world.

We hear a lot of rhetoric about how the United States exports democracy all over the world, but if you really want to understand U.S. influence on other peoples, probably the best places to start are Liberia and the Philippines, which are our two preeminent colonies—I think it's fair to call them that—in Africa and Asia.

We started in Liberia well before 1843, planning to send freed slaves there as one of the "solutions," so to speak, to our slavery problem. Liberia became a U.S. colony in every sense of the word. "Liberia" is the name we gave the country; the capital, Monrovia, and the great port city, Buchanan, are both named after U.S. presidents; the government was organized and put in place directly by the United States; and the national currency is the U.S. dollar. Given these close connections, you'd expect Liberia to be relatively well off. But it would be difficult, even in Africa, to find a people more tormented and endangered and impoverished than Liberia's.

It's the same story in the Philippines, which we conquered during the Philippine-American War—commonly (and inaccurately) called the Spanish-American War. More than a million Filipinos died during that war from violence and dengue fever, a byproduct of the fighting. We had government testimony of widespread use of torture by U.S. troops and of a general giving orders to kill all of the males on Negros Island. Once, that island could feed more than the population of the entire Philippine archipelago. And what's the condition of that island now, after a hundred years of American benevolence? It's owned by twelve families and produces 60 percent of the sugar exported from the Philippines. The children of those who chop the cane starve because their families don't even have enough land to grow their own vegetables. Per capita income in the Philippines ten years ago was less than six hundred dollars. Per capita income in Japan, by contrast, was more than twenty-four thousand dollars. Even the poorest countries in the region have per capita incomes double or triple that of the Philippines.

So what have Liberia and the Philippines gotten out of being de facto colonies of the United States? Poverty, division, confusion, and tyrannical governments. Ferdinand Marcos was our man in Manila. We installed one dictator after another in Liberia.

These two countries represent a small part of our foreign policy, but it's a part where you would expect us to be the most attentive to the well-being of the people. Yet few have suffered more in other parts of the world.

DJ: So how does the U.S. maintain its national self-image as god's gift to the world, the great bastion of democracy?

RC: But we're not a democracy. It's a terrible misunderstanding and a slander to the idea of democracy to call us that. In reality, we're a plutocracy: a government run by the wealthy. Wealth has its way. The concentration of wealth and the division between rich and poor in the U.S. are unequaled anywhere. And think of whom we admire most: the Rockefellers and Morgans, the Bill Gateses and Donald Trumps. Would any moral person accumulate a billion dollars when there are 10 million infants dying of starvation every year? Is that the best thing you can find to do with your time?

DJ: I remember seeing a statistic a few years ago that summed up our priorities for me: for the price of a single B-1 bomber—about $285 million—we could provide basic immunization treatments to the roughly 575 million children in the world who lack them, thus saving 2.5 million lives annually.

RC: Such comparisons have a powerful illustrative impact, implying that if the money weren't spent on bombers, it might be put to good use. The fact is, however, that if the B-1 were canceled, we still wouldn't spend the money on vaccinations, because it wouldn't serve the trade interests of the United States. It's not a part of our vision.

DJ: What, then, is our vision?

RC: Central to our foreign policy has been the active attempt to deprive governments and peoples of the independence that comes from self-sufficiency in the production of food. I've believed for many years that a country that can't produce food for its own people can never really be free. Iran is a good example of this. We overthrew the democratically elected government in Iran and installed the Shah. For twenty-five years, Iran was our surrogate in the Middle East, a hugely important region. After the Shah was overthrown by his own people, CIA chief William Colby called installing the Shah the CIA's proudest achievement and said, "You may think he failed, but for twenty-five years, he served us well."

DJ: Serving us well, in this case, included killing tens of thousands of Iranians just in the year before he left office.

RC: He certainly killed as many as he dared, especially in that last year, 1978. I've always said it was about thirty-seven thousand that year, but we'll never know exactly how many. I think there were two thousand gunned down on Black Friday alone, that August. There were a million people out on the streets that day, and they came through Jaleh Square, many wearing shrouds so that it would be convenient to bury them if they were killed. Huey helicopters fired on them from a hundred feet in the air with fifty-caliber machine guns.

DJ: U.S.-supplied Hueys?

RC: The Hueys were fabricated in Esfahan, Iran, from U.S.-supplied parts. In fact, the fabrication of those Hueys provides an interesting insight into the effects of U.S. influence. In 1500, Esfahan was one of the ten biggest cities in the world, with about half a million people. Culturally, it remained almost pristine until 1955, the year after the Shah took power. As part of the Shah's efforts to fulfill his dream of making Iran the fifth great industrial power in the world, he made Esfahan a center of industrialization. By 1970, the population had increased to 1.5 million, including about eight hundred thousand peasants who had come to live in the slums around this once fabulous city.

Once again, the result of U.S. foreign policy was poverty, anger, hurt, and suffering for the majority. While the canal systems that had supported enough agriculture to feed the population for a couple of millennia were going into decay, causing Iran to import most of its food, the country was buying arms. We sold them more than $22 billion in arms between 1972 and 1977—everything they wanted, except nuclear weapons.

Iran isn't the only Middle Eastern nation dependent upon food imports. Today twenty-two Arab states import more than half of their food. This makes them extremely vulnerable to U.S. economic pressure.

Egypt is a great example of this. It's the second largest U.S. aid recipient in the world, after Israel. Can you imagine what sanctions would do to Cairo? You've got 12 million people living there, 10 million of them in real poverty. The city would be bedlam in ninety days. There would be rebellion in the streets.

The same is true of the other Arab countries. They might think they've got wealth because of their oil, but Iraq has oil, and it hasn't helped that country survive the sanctions. There, sanctions have forced impoverishment on a people who had a quality of life that was by far the best in the region. They had free, universal healthcare and a good educational system. Now they're dying at a rate of about eighteen thousand per month as a direct result of sanctions imposed by the United States in the name of the UN Security Council—the most extreme sanctions imposed in modern times.

The U.S. helped maneuver Iraq into a position where it was one of those twenty-two Arab nations importing more than half its food, and I have always believed that we maneuvered it, as well, into attacking Iran, in that god-awful war that cost a million young men their lives for no purpose. After the collapse of the Shah's regime in 1979, Iraq thought that Iran couldn't defend itself, but didn't take into account the passion that twenty-five years of suffering had created in the population—a passion so strong that you had fifteen-year-old kids running barefoot through swamps into a hail of bullets, and if they got near you, you were dead. They had a pair of pants and a rifle, and that was about it. Meanwhile, Iraq, which was supported by both the Soviet Union and the United States, had artillery it could mount shoulder-to-shoulder and armored vehicles with cannons and machine guns. But the war was still a stalemate.

In any case, by the late 1980s, Iraq was emerging as too powerful a nation in the Middle East. And, fatally for Iraq, it wasn't reliable enough to be our new surrogate. No one would be as good a surrogate for us as the Shah's Iran had been.

So we had to take out Iraq, under the pretense of defending Kuwait. First we bombed Iraq brutally: 110,000 aerial sorties in forty-two days, an average of one every thirty seconds, which dropped 88,500 tons of bombs. (These are Pentagon figures.) We destroyed the infrastructure, to use a cruel euphemism for life-support systems. Take water, for example: we hit reservoirs, dams, pumping stations, pipelines, and purification plants. Some associates and I drove into Iraq at the end of the second week of the war, and there was no running water anywhere. People were drinking water out of the Tigris and Euphrates Rivers.

The Gulf War showed, for the first time, that you could destroy a country without setting foot on its soil. We probably killed a hundred thousand, and our total casualties, according to the Pentagon, were 157—most of them from friendly fire and accidents. The Iraqis caused only minimal casualties. One of those notoriously inaccurate Scud missiles fired toward Saudi Arabia came wobbling down and somehow hit a mess hall tent, killing thirty-seven American soldiers. That's a big chunk of the total casualties right there. We didn't lose a single tank, whereas we destroyed seventeen hundred Iraqi armored vehicles, plinking them with depleted-uranium ammunition and laser guided missiles.

But, as with Vietnam, the sanctions that followed the war have been infinitely more damaging, causing fifteen times the number of casualties. The sanctions against Iraq are genocidal conduct under the law, according to the 1948 United Nations Convention on the Prevention and Punishment of the Crime of Genocide—which, by the way, the United States refused to endorse until 1988 and explicitly refuses to comply with to this day. The sanctions against Iraq have killed more than 1.5 million people, more than half of them children under the age of five, an especially vulnerable segment of the population. Particularly in their first year, children are more susceptible to disease and malnutrition, and to the malnutrition of their mother. Many Iraqi mothers are now so malnourished that they cannot produce milk. They try to give their children sugar water as a substitute, but because the United States destroyed the infrastructure, the water is contaminated; a child can die within forty-eight hours of drinking it. And that child could have been saved by a rehydration tablet that costs less than a penny but is not available because of the sanctions. This is in a country that once produced 15 percent of its own pharmaceuticals. Now it can't even get the raw materials. We have, in an act of will, impoverished a whole population.

DJ: Where do you see such policies taking us?

RC: The great issue of the twenty-first century will be that of the relationship between the rich and poor nations, and of the elimination of some percentage of those whom we consider not only expendable but even undesirable. In many parts of the world, we've got 30 percent of the labor force unemployed and unemployable, and new technology renders them unnecessary. Why, then, from the perspective of capital—and, therefore, from the perspective of U.S. foreign policy—should we support them? Why worry about AIDS in Africa? Why worry about hunger and malnutrition in Bangladesh or Somalia?

DJ: Let me see if I've got this right: from the perspective of those in power, it's desirable to keep the poor alive only insofar as they're useful, and the poor are useful only as labor, or as an excess pool of labor to drive wages down. Beyond that, who needs them?

RC: Yes. It's hard for me to see how we will find meaningful and desirable employment for the poorest segment of the world's population in the face of both ecological degradation and technology's capacity to produce more than we need. How did Dostoevsky put it? "The cruelest punishment that can be inflicted on a person is to force him to work hard at a meaningless task." That may or may not be true, but we do know that such make-work is a form of psychological torture. If your labor isn't needed, if you don't have skills, then what are you worth to a society that won't even bother to vaccinate your children or provide food for your starving infants?

In 1900, half of the labor force in the United States was involved in agriculture. Now it's probably less than 5 percent. In 1900, 80 percent of the labor force in China was involved in food production. When that figure comes down to 10 percent, what are those other 70 percent going to do?

DJ: While we've been talking, I've been thinking about a conversation that took place years ago between Senator George McGovern and Robert Anderson, the president of the military contractor Rockwell International. McGovern asked Anderson if he wouldn't rather build mass transit systems than B-1 bombers. Anderson said he would, but they both knew that there was no chance Congress would appropriate money for public transportation.

RC: They were absolutely right. Capital in the United States would never accept that sort of shift in priorities, for many reasons. The first is that the military is a means of international domination, and any change that might threaten that domination will not be allowed to take place. The second reason is that capital requires continuing, ever expanding demand, and mass transit shrinks demand for automobiles and gas.

When my family moved to Los Angeles when I was a kid, before World War II, it was a paradise. The word "smog" hadn't been invented. There were no such things as freeways. There were mountains, beaches, deserts, and wildlife, and 49 percent of the land in the area was owned by the people of the United States. But the machinery that would destroy that paradise had already been put in motion.

In the 1920s, there had been struggles over whether there would continue to be mass transit in Los Angeles, which at the start of the century had an elaborate streetcar system. But powerful industries—the oil refiners and the automobile manufacturers—fiercely opposed what the people obviously needed. The citizens of Los Angeles were a fast-growing population with long distances to travel, and they needed to get there fast and cheaply. If they'd developed more mass transit, it would have led to an entirely different way of life. Instead, L.A. is now a big, sprawling metropolis with a tangle of freeways and millions of cars, unbelievable in its endless banality and congestion and noise and pollution. But think of what L.A.'s maintaining its excellent mass-transit system would have done to the petrochemical industry and the automobile industry, with all of their accessories—tires, parts, and so on.

Capital promotes activities from which its owners can reap enormous profits. It does not matter if those activities are detrimental to living beings or communities. For example, those in power seem to have an unlimited imagination for conjuring up new excuses to throw money at the military. I was saddened by the almost pathetic naiveté of the people of this country some ten years ago, when we were talking about reaping a "peace dividend."

DJ: Which, of course, we never hear about anymore.

RC: But people believed there would be a peace dividend! Instead, we've devised incredible schemes like SDI—the "Star Wars" Strategic Defense Initiative, which is back again.

DJ: The argument now is that we need SDI to protect us from North Korea.

RC: That's crazy. In the current election, even more than in 1980, when Carter and Reagan were debating the military budget, we saw two candidates vying to prove that they each would provide a stronger defense. But defense from what? In order to keep increasing the demand for military products, we're teaching moral and fiscal insanity. I was in South Africa a couple of weeks ago. After all the people there have suffered, I want to be hopeful for them, yet they just spent over a billion dollars on a bunch of naval vessels.

And we've been consistently sold a bill of goods that has made people believe they've been heroic when they've done terrible things in the name of their country through military actions. I mean, how many of those pilots who bombed Vietnam—even the ones who became prisoners—ever said to themselves, "I wonder what it was like being a Vietnamese villager when I was coming over and dropping those bombs"?

DJ: I kept thinking about that when Senator John McCain used his former prisoner of war status to gain political capital, and I never heard anyone publicly confront him about killing civilians.

I remember once, when I lived in Spokane, Washington, there was a gala event called "A Celebration of Heroes." The headliner was the Gulf War commander Norman Schwarzkopf. Neither the mainstream nor the alternative papers published articles, or even letters to the editor, about Schwarzkopf's war crimes. I think that holding up mass murderers as heroes is as much a problem as holding up the rich.

RC: Violence may not be as harmful as greed in the long run, because it's harder to kill people directly than it is to kill them with sanctions. If you killed that many with bullets, your finger would get tired.

Colin Powell seems to be a compelling figure, but when he was asked during the Gulf War how many Iraqis he thought the United States had killed, his response was—and this is a direct quote—"Frankly, that's a number that doesn't interest me very much." Now, aside from international law, which requires that all participants in war count their enemy dead, that is an extraordinarily inhumane statement. And then you see a fellow like General Barry McCaffrey, whom Clinton later named as his drug czar, coming in and attacking defenseless Iraqi troops as they withdrew, killing several thousand people just like that [snaps his finger.] That's a war crime of the first magnitude. And yet these men are rewarded; they're seen as heroes.

DJ: On another subject, you've also spoken out against our nation's prison system.

RC: One of the most devastating things that has happened in this society—and one of the most ignored—is the stunning growth of the prison system and the use of capital punishment. In the 1960s, a time of maximum domestic turbulence, we were able to bring the government out against the death penalty, leading to a halt in federal executions in 1963. In fact, the first year in U.S. history that there were no executions anywhere was 1968. We also had a moratorium on federal prison construction. The federal prison population was then around twenty thousand. Now, of course, we're building prisons like mad, and the federal prison population is currently about 145,000.

In 1971, prisoners at Attica in New York State rebelled against horrible prison conditions. (Conditions overall are worse today.) The suppression of that rebellion is still the bloodiest day of battle between Americans on American soil since the Civil War: thirty-seven people were killed. At that time, there were fewer than thirteen thousand prisoners in the whole New York prison system; today there are about seventy-five thousand. And the population of the state hasn't risen 5 percent.

Across the country, more than 2 million people are in prison. And in California—which we tend to think of as a trendsetter for the rest of the country—40 percent of African American males between the ages of seventeen and twenty-seven, the most vital years of their lives, are either in prison or under some form of community supervision or probation. What's the reason behind this? It's a means of controlling a major segment of the population. But what does it do to the people?

And what does it mean that we've got politicians like New York City mayor Rudy Giuliani, who insists on sending people to jail for what he calls "quality of life" crimes? What does it mean when 70 percent of young adult African American males have arrest records? What does it mean when so many of these

African Americans have had frightening and damaging experiences with the police? We say we're "the land of the free and the home of the brave," yet we have a prison system unrivaled in the so-called democratic societies, and probably in any society on the planet today. And we're Lord High Executioner.

In the 1960s, South Africa was the world's leading executioner for post-judicial convictions, executing about three hundred people every year—nearly one each day. Most years, all of those executed were black, with the occasional exception of a white who had been convicted of being part of the African National Congress's resistance to apartheid. Back then, the principal argument we made in this country against the death penalty was "We don't want to be like South Africa." Part of the reason that argument worked is that the Civil Rights Movement was ascendant. Another is that people recognized that our executions were racist: for instance, 89 percent of the executions for rape, from the time statistics began to be collected until the Supreme Court abolished executions for rape, were of African American men. And although we don't know the race of all the victims, because those statistics weren't kept, those whose race we have been able to determine were all white. The imposition of the death penalty was—and remains—blatantly racist.

Now South Africa has abolished the death penalty; its constitution prohibits it. Prior to that, its supreme court found the death penalty to be a violation of international and domestic laws. Yet we come on like gangbusters for capital punishment. George W. Bush executed more people than any other governor in the history of the United States.

DJ: You seem to be a good person, yet you filled a major government post. That seems to me an immense contradiction.

RC: If your premise is correct, then that's a terrible indictment of the system. There is something desperately wrong if we don't have the best among us in government service. But it's true; we drive them out.

I joined the Marines during World War II, but a bunch of my buddies were conscientious objectors. Even then, I realized that they were better men than I, that what they did took more courage. I mean, to join the Marines is a piece of cake: all you've got to do is go down to the recruitment center and sign up. But I've watched my conscientious objector friends over the years, and I have to say that they've been very lonely; in some ways, their lives were pretty much wasted. We're social creatures, and these men—boys, really, when they first made that decision—were ostracized for what they did, for following their conscience. And I think that lack of social esteem affected how they perceived themselves.

It seems the best among us often get purged. I have seen many new congresspeople come into Washington, and some of them are just such good people that you can hardly stand it—bright, articulate people who care about issues. But it seems that, if they get reelected a few times, they start to sit around and scowl and drink too much, and their families break up. If you see this happen enough times, you begin to realize the enormous corrupting power of our political system. To be successful in it, you might have to make compromises that will cause you not to like yourself very much. And then you'll have to compensate for that in some way. You can become excessively ambitious, or greedy, or corrupt, or something else, but something's got to happen, because if you don't like yourself, what do you do?

Young people often ask me if they should go to law school, and I always say, "If you're not tough, you'll get your values beaten out of you, and you'll move into a kind of fee-grabbing existence where your self-esteem will depend on how much you bill per hour and what kind of clients you bring in to the law firm. You might find yourself turning into nothing but a money mill."

If we are to significantly change our culture, we need to recognize that we are held in thrall by two desperately harmful value patterns. One is the glorification of violence. We absolutely, irrationally, insanely glorify violence. We often think that we enjoy watching the good guys kill the bad guys, but the truth is that we enjoy watching the kill itself.

The other value is materialism. We are the most materialistic people who have ever lived. We value things over children. Indeed, the way we show how much we value children is by giving them things, to the point where a mother's self-esteem depends on whether she's the first in her neighborhood to get her child some new toy.

I think the hardest part for us is to break through the illusory world that the media create. Television is a big part of our reality. Children spend more time watching TV than they do in school or participating in any other activity. And television is a preacher of materialism above all else. It tells us constantly to want things. More money is spent on commercials than on the entertainment itself. And that entertainment is essentially hypnotic.

I think often of the Roman poet Juvenal's line about "bread and circuses." All these distractions that now fill our lives are an unprecedented mechanism of social control, because they occupy so much of our time that we don't reason, we don't imagine, and we don't use our senses. We walk though our day mesmerized, never questioning, never thinking, never appreciating. From this process we emerge a synthetic vessel without moral purpose, with no notion in our head or our heart of what is good for people, of what builds a healthier, happier, more loving society.

You began this interview by asking me about U.S. foreign policy, and I said that it's been a failure. Here is the standard by which I would judge any foreign or domestic policy: has it built a healthier, happier, more loving society, both at home and abroad? The answer, in our case, is no on both counts.

DJ: So what do we do?

RC: I think the solution relies on the power of the idea, and the power of the word, and on a belief that, in the end, the ultimate power resides in the people.

In discussing the effects of U.S. foreign policy, we've been talking about only one part of the story. Another part is resistance—the power of the people. We saw that in the Philippines, when Marcos was deposed in a nonviolent revolution, and we saw that in Iran, when the Shah's staggering power was overcome, as well, by a nonviolent revolution.

Of course, just getting rid of Marcos or the Shah is not the end of the story. People sometimes think that, after the glorious revolution, everybody is going to live happily ever after. But it doesn't work that way. What they've gone through in the struggle has divided them, confused them, and driven them to extremes of desperation.

I think what all of this means is that we each have to do our own part, and become responsible, civic-minded citizens. We have to realize that we won't be happy unless we try to do our part. And if a small portion of us simply do our part, that will be enough. If even 1 percent of the people of this country could break out of the invisible chains, they could bring down this military-industrial complex—this tyranny of corporations, this plutocracy—overnight. That's all it would take: 1 percent of the people.

We also have to realize that we're going to be here only one time, and we've got to enjoy life, however hard it is. To miss the opportunity for joy is to miss life. Any fool can be unhappy; in fact, we make whole industries out of being unhappy, because happy people generally make lousy consumers. It's interesting to see how the poor understand all of this better than the rich. This morning, I was in court over in Brooklyn, representing a group of Romany—they're often called Gypsies, but they don't like to be called that—who were claiming recognition for losses in the Holocaust. The Romany lost 1.5 million people, yet nobody pays any attention to their claims. In fact, last year, the city of Munich, Germany, enacted legislation that is almost a verbatim reproduction of 1934 legislation prohibiting Romany from coming into the city; they'll be arrested if they do. The Romany might be the most endangered people on the planet— even more so than the 200 million indigenous people around the globe. They are fugitives everywhere they go, persecuted everywhere. Yet, like the traditional indigenous peoples, they are people of exceptional joy. They sing and dance and have fun. They can't see life as so much drudgery.

I saw that same joy among the civil rights protesters in the 1960s. Watching them sing as they marched, I couldn't help but realize that you feel better when you're doing something you feel is right—no matter how hard it is.

STEPHEN SCHWARTZ

Interview conducted on
November 6, 2000, at the
Bulletin of Atomic Scientists
in Chicago, Illinois.

"Nuclear weapons and democracy can't coexist," declares Stephen Schwartz. He came to that conclusion after researching the cost of the U.S. nuclear weapons program: $5.5 trillion between 1940 and 1996. These weapons have "sucked the economy dry." But the full costs are even greater. Nuclear weapons require a policy of silence, obfuscation, and lies, and the result has been a "massive erosion of trust in the American government by its citizens." Once the government committed to a policy of deterrence, the factual information about the risks of nuclear production, testing, deployments, and accidents had to be hidden. Schwartz says, "If the public had understood that testing nuclear weapons in Nevada meant that fallout would drift across the country and injure and even kill many people, no citizens in their right minds would have stood for that."

And yet the essence of democracy is an informed public. We can't have a true debate about our national priorities without all the facts about nuclear weapons, including their costs, their dangers, and their possible uses. Many military officers believe nuclear weapons "are not usable in any military sense of the word"— they're simply too destructive to use. The U.S. could achieve its foreign policy goals using political, diplomatic, and economic means, with the conventional military as a last resort. And we could fund instead the social infrastructure of hospitals and schools rather than risky weapons that are "irrelevant to national defense."

The worst news is that even though it's dropped from public consciousness, "nuclear reality is still in place." The Cold War may be over, but America's nuclear war plans, weapons, and policies have not changed. If anything, things have gotten worse, as depleted uranium is spread around the world, as the threat of nuclear weapons fails to recede: as this book goes to press, North Korea is threatening once again to attack South Korea, and the mainstream corporate press mentions the "U.S. nuclear shield" as part of South Korea's defense. Schwartz ends with an urgent plea for action: "Stand up, speak as citizens, and make certain that the government cannot ignore your voice." Always good advice if democracy, and indeed our planet, have any hope for survival.

Schwartz is editor of *The Nonproliferation Review*. He has served as publisher and executive director of the *Bulletin of the Atomic Scientists*, guest scholar and project director with the Foreign Policy Studies program at the Brookings Institution, legislative director for Nuclear Campaigns with Greenpeace USA, and associate director of the Council on Nuclear Affairs. Mr. Schwartz is the author of *Nuclear Security Spending: Assessing Costs, Examining Priorities* (Carnegie Endowment for International Peace) and the editor and co-author of *Atomic Audit: The Costs and Consequences of U.S. Nuclear Weapons Since 1940* (Brookings Institution Press).

Derrick Jensen: How much has the U.S. nuclear weapons program cost?

Stephen Schwartz: Well, in late 1993 we started the book *Atomic Audit* in order to answer that question. It took us about four years. One reason it took so long is that we soon discovered this was the first time anybody had actually attempted to calculate this. We kept thinking the figures must be hidden away somewhere in the government, and if we could find them we could just pull them out and update them. But it turns out that the government never even kept track of the costs.

All that said, our best guess, and this really should be looked at more as a floor than a ceiling, is that between 1940, when the U.S. made its first payment for work connected with the development of nuclear weapons, through 1996, when we stopped counting, the United States government spent about $5.5 trillion. That's in adjusted 1996 dollars, so we've removed the effects of inflation, meaning a dollar in 1950 in our study is worth the same as a dollar in 1990. Since 1996 the government has spent approximately $35 billion dollars a year. You can do the math and see what's been spent since then.

We also looked at the incurred costs for the nuclear weapons program—things we knew the government would be spending money on in the future and that we could estimate with relative precision—things like cleaning up nuclear waste from past nuclear weapons production, compensating people harmed by nuclear weapons testing activities, dismantling surplus nuclear weapons, and storing surplus nuclear weapons material. When you add all those costs in, you get up to about $5.8 trillion, which is obviously an enormous amount of money any way you look at it. If you were to dole it out to everybody living in the country in 1996, it would have come to almost twenty-two thousand dollars per person, enough to buy everybody a nice new car. Or you could stack the money up to the moon and nearly back again in one dollar bills.

A lot of people don't like those comparisons. They say, "Well, if you spread that money out among all the people who were alive over that fifty-five years, it ends up being something like a dollar a day, so what's the big deal?" Well, the big deal is that we didn't know what we were spending, and we ended up spending way too much. The nuclear weapons program is the third most expensive program the U.S. government has ever undertaken, behind only all other national defense programs including World War II—about $13.2 trillion—and social security, which at this point is sort of a quasi-government program, at about $7.9 trillion. The nuclear weapons program amounts to eleven percent of all government expenditures between 1940 and 1996, an average of nearly $98 billion per year.

When the book came out, that shocked a lot of people. It didn't, unfortunately, shock enough politicians. We were expecting a big reaction on Capitol Hill, but it didn't happen. There was almost total silence.

DJ: Considering the fiscal horrors that characterize the military, in some ways it doesn't surprise me that no one counted the costs.

SS: It surprised us. And the interesting thing was that the Air Force initially did try to conduct an audit of the program, in response, ironically, to criticism from Congress that they weren't spending enough money on nuclear weapons. In about 1950 a member of Congress did some creative math—what George W. Bush would call *fuzzy math*—and calculated the government was only spending something like three cents out of every military dollar for nuclear weapons. He said this amount was "unreasonably and imprudently small," and that the U.S. "must go all-out" on the nuclear weapons program.

DJ: How was the math fuzzy?

SS: It didn't include a whole bunch of other costs, such as the delivery systems— the means of getting the weapons to their target—which at that point was strictly Strategic Air Command bomber aircraft. And it only included some but not all of the costs of the Atomic Energy Commission.

Today you'll see the same sort of fuzzy math, although different tricks are used. Figures put out by the Defense Department show that we're spending a relatively small amount of money, but all they count is a portion of the delivery systems. They don't count any other costs of the Department of Energy—which took over for the Atomic Energy Commission—the costs of overseeing the warheads, and so on.

Part of the problem was that the military budget wasn't set up to discriminate between nuclear and non-nuclear spending, and Air Force auditors and other people found it too difficult to pull the costs apart, because they were in some senses interconnected. So they just gave up, and said to Congress, "You'll have to trust us when we say we're spending enough money."

Another reason there was no accountability was a real lack of inquisitiveness on the part of the elected representatives who were allocating this money on a regular basis—annually and sometimes even semi-annually, when there were emergency spending bills—to the tune of tens or hundreds of billions of dollars. Now, the people doling out the money had a general sense of the scale of the program. They knew, for example, how many factories were producing nuclear weapons, they knew more or less how many nuclear weapons were being tested, and eventually they found out how many weapons were in the arsenal, although even that was a closely held secret for many years. And of course they knew what the government was spending on things like bomber aircraft, submarines, and all that. But no one had ever tried to piece the whole puzzle together.

Lately I've been seeing everything through the lens of home renovations, probably because I've been renovating my home, and it's occurred to me that the way the country handled the nuclear weapons program would be analogous to looking at only the costs of the subcontractor who did the plumbing, or the electrical work, or the framing, yet never bothering to look at the entire cost. You may have an impression, but that's all it is.

DJ: How did we come to spend so much money?

SS: Nuclear weapons are closely interconnected, of course, with the Cold War. If we hadn't had the kind and duration of Cold War that we did, the scope and cost of the program would have been far different than it was.

DJ: Didn't we end up in a feedback loop, where the U.S. . . . ?

SS: We did something, the Soviet Union responded, we responded to their response, and that's the arms races in a nutshell. Intelligence officials seemed to systematically fail to understand, as did policy makers, that if you build a thousand Minuteman missiles, you were deluding yourself into expecting the

Russians to hold up their hands and say, "Well, gosh we can't compete with that. We give up." There was going to be a response, and then that response would be perceived not as a response to our initiative, but as the Soviets ratcheting up to the next level and saying, "We're coming after you. We're threatening you." This then would alarm us, and lead to a further response.

So, fear was certainly a great factor. Fear of the Soviet Union, and later fear of China. People were concerned about the future. Would the "godless communists" take over? Or would the United States prevail? Absent any compelling evidence at that time that nuclear weapons wouldn't have worked, people probably thought they were a good thing to have. You have to remember that from within the perspective of those who most strongly supported the nuclear weapons program, we won World War II essentially because of the use of nuclear weapons. I don't fully subscribe to that argument, but it's important to recognize it. And therefore, from that perspective, why would we give up the best weapon in our arsenal, the one that could actually make all other wars obsolete?

Another reason for the size of the program was its secrecy. Not only, as I said, were members of Congress kept uninformed—and sometimes kept themselves deliberately uninformed—but a great deal of information was not available to the general public. I'm not here arguing that the general public needs to know exactly how every nuclear weapon is screwed together, but the public not only deserves but *needs* to know the basics of the program, such as where the weapons are based, what sorts of strategies the government is considering, whether the weapons are to be used mainly as a deterrent or to actually fight wars. The public needs to know how much the weapons cost. And certainly the public needs to know what dangers are associated with building, testing, and employing these weapons. Yet all of those things have been off-limits. The government as a whole, and officials, scientists, and members of the military as individuals have said, "Trust us. We're defending the country. We'll do what's right." And for many years the public did trust them, until the understanding started creeping out that there were some serious problems associated with nuclear weapons.

Another reason for the outlandish size of the nuclear weapons program is, to be honest, arbitrary decision-making. Officials regularly testified before Congress or made public statements that this or that number of missiles would be enough to ensure deterrence, enough to fight off the Soviets in Europe, or whatever. I don't know I'd go so far as to say those numbers were made up, but it often seems they were pulled out of a hat. They certainly weren't the result of any sort of carefully concluded analysis about exactly what was required. Secretary of Defense Robert McNamara later acknowledged that the numbers they came up with were the result of a "visceral feeling" as to how many would be sufficient. And the numbers were often the result of interservice rivalry, where if the Air Force got a certain number of missiles, well, the Army had to have that many, too. They were often the result of pork-barrel politics, where members of Congress requested more than they felt the country needed because it provided jobs for their constituents. Why do we have twenty-one B-2 bombers instead of twenty? In 1996 President Clinton authorized the conversion of one test aircraft to an operational aircraft, not because the Air Force wanted or needed it, but because it created jobs in California, and Clinton needed the electoral votes.

There are two other factors I think are at least as important, if not more so, than these others. The first was that until the early 1950s, the ability of the United States and the Atomic Energy Commission to manufacture large numbers of nuclear weapons was constrained by the relatively small amount of fissile material—plutonium and highly enriched uranium—available to go into those weapons. Now, in the wake of the Korean War, China being taken over by the Communists, and revelations about Klaus Fuchs and the Rosenbergs, Congress authorized an enormous amount of money for production facilities. As much money was authorized just in 1951, for example, as had been spent during the entire Manhattan Project during World War II. The result was that by the late 1950s we had an enormous increase in the production of highly enriched uranium and plutonium, and by the mid-1960s we had such a huge surplus of highly enriched uranium that President Johnson stopped production.

The government was also getting a surplus of plutonium at that point. That overcapacity allowed the government to build as many warheads as it wanted.

There is one more key factor, which is that the military never had to pay for the warheads. Although the Atomic Energy Commission budget was part of the overall military budget, the different services themselves—Army, Navy, Air Force, Marines—weren't responsible for footing the bill for this or that warhead. This means that there was no incentive *not* to ask for a nuclear weapon when a conventional one might do. And there was no incentive not to ask for as many nuclear weapons as you could possibly get, because somebody else would take care of the costs. A number of people have said, in retrospect, that had the Air Force been forced to pay for all of the warheads for all of those Minuteman missiles, and had the Army been forced to pay for all of the thousands of warheads deployed in Europe and Korea, the arsenal would have been far smaller than it was.

Because the different services didn't have to pay for their own weapons, we saw some very interesting proposals, like that put forward by General James Gavin, head of Army research and development, who testified on Capitol Hill in 1956 and 1957 that the Army alone required 151,000 warheads, because it might need up to 423 in a single day of intense combat. Keep in mind that the government only ever built about 70,000 warheads. And at the maximum back in 1958 and 1959, the government was producing about six to seven thousand per year. So it's just a fantastic figure. After the book was published, I stumbled across another figure: the Joint Chiefs of Staff argued in the late 1950s that by the early 1960s we ought to have something like 75,000 warheads in the U.S. arsenal. The Joint Chiefs of Staff provided no explanation of how that figure was arrived at, or what the breakdown would be.

One of the questions we get asked a lot is, "If the government spent too much money and had too many weapons, what was the right amount? Give us a figure." And I can't do that. Nobody can, because deterrence is completely subjective. You're the Soviet Union, I'm the United States. I fear you, I don't understand you, you're way the hell over on the other side of the ocean, and I don't get what's going on with you. And I demonize you. So, whereas ten nuclear weapons might be enough to make me quake in my boots and think, "I'm not going to mess with these people," I believe that might not be enough for you. You might not value life as much as I do. You may have a completely different concept of what constitutes acceptable destruction. So I'll need to be ready to launch twenty or thirty nuclear weapons against you. That, in a very oversimplified way, is the kind of thinking that went on.

The next step in the argument goes: well, we won the Cold War, so obviously it was worth it. But that misses the point in two fundamental ways. The first is that we didn't know what we were spending. Let's consider nuclear deterrence like insurance. What person would buy home insurance and not pay attention to how much it costs? And second, what person would buy home insurance that actually *increases* the risk that the house will be destroyed? The truth is that nuclear deterrence is not a safeguard. The bottom line of nuclear deterrence is: "I'm going to blow you up and I'm going to blow myself up, too." When I tell audiences this a few people giggle, but others realize that this truly is a dangerous thing.

Nuclear weapons are always off somewhere else, particularly today. I think most people think they don't exist anymore, or if they do, they're in North Korea's hands, or Pakistan's. But nobody thinks about our weapons, nobody thinks about all the weapons left in Russia at the end of the Cold War that are still there, still pointed at us, notwithstanding all the talk for years about them being pointed somewhere else.

Creating and deploying these nuclear weapons has created a very real risk for us and for the rest of the world. We don't just have them sitting around in warehouses somewhere ready to pull out if things get nasty somewhere. In the 1960s, they were on bomber aircraft constantly flying around the globe, armed and ready to go. The whole *Dr. Strangelove/Fail-Safe* scenario was real. And they were on submarines patrolling the oceans. They still are. They were on high alert in Europe and elsewhere, ready to go, quick launch alert, sometimes essentially without safeguards; the only safeguard was the pilot in the plane, whom we were hoping was a sane individual who wouldn't take off on his own accord and bomb Kiev just because he was having a bad day. It was a *really* risky strategy. People still don't understand how dangerous that was.

DJ: Not only was there the possibility of *Dr. Strangelove*, but there were any number of accidents.

SS: A lot of bombs fell out of airplanes. Either the airplanes crashed and the bombs fell out of them, or the bombs fell out of the airplanes and *then* the airplanes crashed. Or submarines went to the bottom of the ocean. There's a bomb off the coast of Georgia that's now creating a stir forty plus years after it fell—or rather was dropped, deliberately—into the mouth of the Savannah River. Why are people worrying about it now? Not because the government was particularly forthcoming, but because a documentary filmmaker has been helping to push the story by saying this is something people need to know about. It may not present a serious risk to anybody in terms of exploding—the filmmaker and I happen to disagree on that: I doubt that's a likely possibility given how long the weapon has been underwater, while he thinks it could happen—but there's certainly a risk of contamination.

I also think it's important for people to know that these weapons are not a thing of the past. They're still out there, ready to go. They're not on planes circling the globe anymore. The government stopped that after a couple of B-52s crashed in Spain and Greenland. And certainly the number of weapons has gone down. Today there are around ten thousand for the U.S., and ten thousand for the Russians. Of course I think that reduction is all to the good. But the policies and strategies that govern how those weapons will be used are still very much Cold War policies. The government still plans on obliterating Russia with thousands of nuclear warheads if the U.S. president decides to launch a nuclear attack. And he still has the authority and capability to do that. The government still plans around him doing that, and for all intents and purposes, the military and nuclear weapons laboratories are intent on keeping that capability for decades to come.

DJ: What are the effects of all of this secrecy on democracy?

SS: Nuclear weapons and democracy can't coexist. Nuclear weapons require secrecy in order to do what you need them to do. As soon as people truly realize how dangerous and expensive they are, they go away.

When you really dig into the history of nuclear weapons, and their present usage, when you delve into the accidents, and into what nuclear weapons mean to the people of this country and the world, you can see very clearly that the primary motivator for governmental decisions about whether and how to release information about nuclear weapons production, testing, deployment, accidents, and so forth, has been to make certain that nothing will constrain the ability of the military to carry out its deterrent mission by having an arsenal of nuclear weapons. This means a lot of silence, a lot of obfuscation, and a lot of lies. My feeling has been for a long time that if U.S. nuclear policy cannot withstand public and Congressional scrutiny of the kind routinely given other federal programs—welfare, environmental programs, agriculture, farm subsidies, whatever—then we need to seriously reconsider why we have those weapons. If the military and the government cannot justify this publicly in a way that balances risks to the public versus the presumed benefits created by having a nuclear deterrent, then we ought to revisit the policy.

I have to say that I don't like being pegged as anti-nuclear, because that's a huge umbrella, and it's not what *Atomic Audit* is about at all. It's really more of an insistence that the American public be allowed to make informed decisions.

The book was in part an attempt to get people to think about nuclear weapons in a way they've not thought of them before. People don't generally think about nuclear weapons in terms of them being too expensive. When they think about them at all, usually it's in terms of the feeling, "I'm going to die, these weapons are going to kill me, they're going to obliterate the planet." Obliterating the planet is, of course, a bad thing. But nobody pays attention to the more mundane reality that these weapons suck the economy dry. Think of all the things we could do with that understanding. If we're told that education is our number one priority, what happens when we compare how much the federal government spends on education to how much it spends on nuclear weapons? If you think there's something wrong with this country economically, or with our education system, or that we're not spending enough on general sciences, look at where the money is going. You can reallocate those funds, but unless and until people understand where the money is going, we can't have that kind of informed debate.

DJ: It's almost a cliché to remark that there's always money for the military, yet you've got to scratch and claw to get funding for anything that serves the needs of living, breathing people.

SS: We've got plenty of quotes from members of Congress saying that their number one priority must be to provide for the national defense, because if you don't have a strong defense nothing else matters. I would argue that the kinds of infrastructures we provide in this country—everything from the educational infrastructure to the transportation and electrical infrastructures to our constitutional democracy itself—are far more important to the health and vitality and longevity of this country than are nuclear weapons.

In fact, I think nuclear weapons are today irrelevant to national defense. I think the same was true for much of the Cold War. They're too big, they're too dangerous to use, they're self-deterring. I have a hard time conceiving of a situation where a sane president would authorize use of nuclear weapons on any scale, except perhaps in a fit of madness or as a response to some sort of massive attack from the other side.

Even the military has been phasing out nuclear weapons. At peak in 1967 and 1968, the government had more than thirty-two thousand deployed all at once. The number has been coming down ever since then. Why is that? Is it because of arms control agreements? Well, no, not until very recently. Is it because the public has been out there protesting and criticizing? Well, no, not very much. Although I don't want to speak ill of the role of public protests, I don't think they've had a major impact on the number of nuclear weapons.

DJ: What has?

SS: The military. Only *after* the frenzied buildup of the 1950s and 1960s, where basically anything that could be nuclearized was, did members of the military start trying to assess how nuclear weapons would be used. The Davy Crockett is a good example of this. It's a tiny nuclear howitzer, a rocket-propelled nuclear warhead that was supposed to be used against Soviet troops en masse. It was the smallest fission bomb the government ever developed. But it wasn't until after the government had built thousands of these things at great cost that the Army started conducting test exercises. It turned out that the weapon was too inaccurate to be used, and also created enormous security risks because you'd have to delegate launching authority to a very low level in order for it to be fired without being overrun in the first wave of battle. That's just one example. The military looked at what it had done and said, "We don't need nuclear depth charges and nuclear torpedoes and nuclear landmines and nuclear air to ground and ground to air and air to air and ground to ground missiles." They started removing nuclear missiles one by one, slowly at first, and then somewhat more rapidly, to the point where in 1991 when George Bush removed almost all of the non-strategic nuclear weapons from Europe and Korea, there wasn't a peep out of the military. In fact the Navy was thrilled because suddenly they were going to be able to use the space on their ships and submarines that had been previously occupied by nukes for conventional weapons. And they wouldn't be burdened by all the required extra training and security.

If you talk to military officers—and I have—even the ones who don't necessarily subscribe to my belief that nuclear deterrence is useless often believe the government has too many weapons, and believe nuclear weapons are not usable in any military sense of the word. Unfortunately, that view doesn't get propelled up to the presidential level, where we've had extremely weak leadership in this area over the last ten years. We had enormous opportunities in 1992 and 1993 when President Clinton took office, but nothing happened, I think in part because of his shaky relationship with the military, but also just his general unwillingness to take this issue on.

DJ: These days we keep hearing we need nukes to stop so-called rogue states . . .

SS: . . . North Korea, Iran, Iraq. I don't think nuclear weapons offer anything with regard to those countries. I can't imagine a circumstance where a president would authorize the use of nuclear weapons against Iran or Iraq, knowing first of all that even the smallest nuclear weapons would devastate an enormous area and kill a large number of people, and second that fallout would drift over countries that aren't enemies. Fallout doesn't just stop at the border. Plus there are enormous political—not to mention environmental—implications of using nuclear weapons, and I just don't think anyone will be foolish enough to use them.

It's absurd anyway. Here we have the most powerful country in the world, spending more money on its military than all of its competitors combined, and it needs nuclear weapons to protect itself against Iraq? Clearly conventional weapons were more than enough to deal with Iraq.

Now, military specialists will tell us that there may be areas of the world where it's difficult to fight with conventional capabilities, and give that as a reason why nuclear weapons labs have come up with the notion of developing a new generation of micronukes that would be larger than the largest conventional weapons but much smaller than the smallest nukes. They say these would be usable weapons.

DJ: Which takes us back in a sense to the Davy Crockett.

SS: It does bring us full circle. And it's incredibly foolish and counterproductive. The government can accomplish what it wants by political, diplomatic, and economic means, and if that fails it has conventional military capabilities unrivaled in the world. It would be far better for us to focus on eliminating the incentive for countries to get nukes by demythologizing nuclear weapons, and eliminating the illusion that they actually have value. By holding on to them ourselves, by pretending or believing nuclear weapons can be useful or beneficial, we create the very situation that causes other countries to seek to acquire them.

DJ: One of the difficulties I have with even talking about reducing or eliminating nuclear weapons is the presumption that reasoned argument will win the day.

SS: Whether or not it will, you can't even begin to have a reasonable discussion without the facts, and we've been missing the facts on these issues for fifty plus years.

But I agree with you that reason often takes a backseat. The whole controversy at the Smithsonian over the Enola Gay exhibit is a perfect example of that. The Enola Gay was the plane that dropped the atomic bomb on Hiroshima. A few years ago the Smithsonian decided to put up an exhibit about it. Unfortunately, the exhibit was derailed by politics, and the unwillingness of the Smithsonian's Congressional overseers to let historical facts get in the way of the story they wanted told: they wanted a rah-rah commemorative focusing on how the atomic bomb won the war, with nothing in there about what those bombs did to the people on the ground. If you go back and review not only the Congressional testimony but a lot of the press coverage, you'll discover that this thing was distorted from day one by people who very clearly aimed to sabotage a rendering of history that did not accord to their worldview. That's unfortunate, because as so often happens, the ultimate losers were the American public. Everybody who went to the museum saw a much scaled-back exhibition, which basically consisted of a chunk of fuselage with a small plaque that provided no context, no understanding, no real information.

DJ: Which is typical for how the government has all along handled information relating to nuclear weapons.

SS: Of course the whole history of the Cold War is one in which the government controlled pretty much all of the information about nuclear weapons. One result of this secrecy has been a massive erosion of trust in the American government by its citizens. Before the early to mid-1950s people were more willing to take the government's word when it said citizens should keep their mouths shut and not ask too many questions. But as people began to realize that they were being misled—in ways detrimental to their health and to the health of the economy and environment—people started to rise up to stem some of the larger abuses of the government's nuclear weapons program. And they lost faith. I sometimes wonder how much of the general erosion of public trust in the government we can blame on the government's secrecy about nuclear weapons, and I wonder how things might have turned out had the government been completely open from the get-go.

But that couldn't have happened. When you look at discussions inside the government about nuclear weapons you sense that politicians and bureaucrats have always had a strong feeling that if they told the public the truth, the public would oppose the programs. And of course they were right, because if the public had understood that testing nuclear weapons in Nevada, for example, meant that fallout would drift across the country and kill lots of people, no citizens in their right minds would have stood for that. Or if they had been told that nuclear weapons pose risks of accidental detonation or leakage, they would certainly not have wanted these weapons kept near their homes. The result is a Kafkaesque reality in which people are told, "These weapons are very important. They are necessary for protecting *you*. But we can't tell you too much about them, because if we do, you won't let us continue to protect you with these weapons."

Unfortunately that situation has largely continued today, when there continues to be a relatively low understanding of nuclear weapons issues in this country, partly because of the secrecy over the years, and partly because people have been told that nuclear weapons are just too complicated for them to understand. But nuclear policies are not that complicated. And I would argue that it's absolutely essential for people to understand them if we're going to have any semblance of a democracy, and if we believe that the essence of democracy is an informed public. A public that is not informed about some of the most basic issues affecting the state of the country, affecting the government's pocketbook, for example, or the national welfare, is not going to be able to make informed choices. And if you can't make informed choices you're probably going to end up making the wrong choices. That can be very expensive and dangerous.

DJ: I think this is all really interesting, but with the Cold War over, isn't it all just old news?

SS: I wish. I'd like nothing more than to retire our Doomsday Clock. Unfortunately that's an event that will be many years in the future, maybe not even in my lifetime.

DJ: Another way to ask this, I suppose, is why should Americans care?

SS: Because the Russians still have about two thousand nuclear warheads pointed at us, and we still have about two thousand pointed at them, and either head of state can, in the space of a couple of minutes, order the instant incineration of either country. The Cold War is over, but both sides still have all of their weapons, and they still have in place all of their policies. The threat is still there; it's just been submerged. It's not covered in the news media anymore, because for the most part world leaders aren't talking about it anymore.

Proliferation concerns are still there, too, and although the veneer of world affairs has in many ways changed, the nuclear reality is still in place. The war plans are still there, the weapons are still there, the policies are still there. And they will remain there for quite some time. With all of those weapons and plans come of course not only the risk that one country or another will deliberately or accidentally launch an attack, but by maintaining those arsenals today— particularly with the United States doing so—we send a message to every country in the world that feels threatened by a neighbor or some sort of group within its borders that the answer to its security problems lies with nuclear weapons.

DJ: I don't understand.

SS: If the United States—the most economically prosperous, the most militarily powerful country in the world—feels it requires nuclear weapons to defend itself or its allies, then who am I—India, Pakistan, China, North Korea, Iran, Iraq, and so on—to not seek nuclear weapons as well? My problems are much more immediate in terms of time and distance. India and Pakistan are fighting an active war over Kashmir. And they both have nuclear weapons.

We're at cross-purposes. We want the world to do as we say, and not as we do. That's a policy that never really worked during the Cold War, it didn't work in the immediate post-Cold War period, and it won't work today.

These nuclear nonproliferation treaties have done a world of good. Going on forty years ago President Kennedy predicted that there would by now be thirty nuclear powers in the world, yet there are only eight, in great measure because of the Nuclear Nonproliferation Treaty, in which countries without nuclear weapons promised not to develop them. But there was another stipulation of those agreements that we don't talk about—don't think about—very often, which is that the nuclear powers at the time—the United States, Soviet Union, Britain, and later France and China–would each seek to eliminate their nuclear arsenals and seek global nuclear disarmament. No timetable was set, but that was their commitment. Ever since 1968 when the treaty was signed, the non-nuclear countries have been waiting for us to fulfill our end of the bargain.

I think quite frankly that thanks to the first Bush administration and then the Clinton administration, we have already lost the opportunity to see effective and complete nuclear disarmament, because we never insisted on sitting down with Russia and talking about exactly how many nuclear weapons they had at the end of the Cold War, and where they were, with the result being that if we ever decide to go down to anything below about a thousand or fifteen hundred warheads—the point where it becomes important to know exactly how many weapons there are—we'll never be sure that we got them all, because there has never been an official inventory.

DJ: Isn't it also true that Clinton not only didn't pursue nonproliferation, but that he boosted research and development on nuclear weapons?

SS: Oh, yes, and that's continuing. There are a number of bad signs concerning the United States nuclear program.

In the mid-1990s the government envisioned the Stockpile Stewardship Program. The idea was that the government would no longer test nuclear weapons, instead conducting simulated testing via this program. It was supposed to cost about $4 billion a year for ten years to build up the infrastructure to do this, and then it would take some amount of money annually to operate it. But very quickly the budget went to $4.5 billion, and now it's over $5 billion a year. One of the interesting things about this is that the United States historically spent about $4 billion in adjusted 2001 dollars on testing. This means that now the government now spends a billion dollars a year *more* than it did on average during the Cold War, when the government was sometimes building thousands of warheads per year, and testing several dozen per year. Now, we're not building or testing any warheads, but we're spending even more money! One could actually make the argument on economic grounds that the government should resume production and testing of nuclear weapons, because it's less expensive than what we're doing today!

Of course I wouldn't make that argument, but it was obvious under Clinton and was even more obvious under the Bush administration that even more money was going to be dumped into that and other nuclear weapons programs.

Another very bad sign is that the U.S. government has talked about developing new types of nuclear weapons. And there are plans afoot—quiet, to be sure—to resume testing and production of weapons. The new weapons, as I mentioned before, would be very small, maybe taking out a building as opposed to a city, with the reasoning being that these weapons would be more usable.

Yet another bad sign was the way that the Bush administration was able to co-opt many of the arguments of the disarmament and peace communities to rationalize further nuclearization. They said, "It is immoral and unjustifiable for us to continue to threaten mass extinction through nuclear weapons. We need a better way." And guess what? Their better way began with abolishing what they called a relic of the Cold War, the 1972 Anti-Ballistic Missile treaty, which limited the amount and types of defenses against ballistic missiles.

We're well on our way to becoming the ultimate rogue state, the sort of country that can basically do anything it wants anywhere it wants anytime it wants without having to worry about consulting with enemies or even allies. The way that the Bush administration spun its desire to get rid of the ABM treaty was unconscionable. And the media and most of us let them get by with it. The ABM treaty was not designed to perpetuate nuclear proliferation, as Bush would have had us think. The treaty was designed to prevent an even more dangerous world than was already on its way, where one or both sides would have defenses, and then both sides would continue to build more offensive weapons to overwhelm or outwit or underfly those defenses so that some would always get through and deterrence would be preserved. Both the United States and the Soviet Union understood that this was a never-ending process that would be very expensive and ultimately very dangerous. And since neither the Soviet Union nor the United States wanted to stem the problem by capping the number of offensive weapons that could be built, or reducing those weapons, they decided to limit defenses, and left limiting offenses for another day. That's the history of the ABM treaty, and if you understand that, then suddenly it becomes much less obvious that National Missile Defense is the answer to all of our problems. But if you don't get that, then you would have been more willing to go along with people in the government who thought this was a super-duper idea.

DJ: Tell me more about missile defenses, or SDI, or Star Wars, or whatever its current name is.

SS: I don't know that there really is a name. The government was calling it National Missile Defense, and then the administration dropped National because they were trying to encourage European support, and the Europeans said, "Why should we support something that's national?"

The notion behind a Missile Defense system is that we'll create a system that will stop ballistic missiles before they hit the United States. Technically it is an extremely difficult, if not impossible, situation, to intercept missiles traveling fifteen thousand miles per hour, with less than a half-hour from launch to detonation. The United States has spent more than $131 billion on Missile Defense and its predecessors. Estimates of the cost of implementing one—once the money has been spent to develop it—run from $60 billion to $500 billion.

One of the problems with the Missile Defense system is that it is aimed at targeting the wrong threat. Proponents of Missile Defenses talk about all of the countries in the world that are building ballistic missiles, but they neglect to point out—even though they know full well—that most of those missiles are very short range and couldn't possibly reach the United States. The only countries that can attack us with long range missiles today are Russia, whom we say is not an enemy, and whom we say the system is not designed against, and China, which has something like twenty warheads that can reach part of the western United States. That's it. The only countries that have missiles with ranges greater than a thousand kilometers and active missile development programs that pose any threat to us are Iran and North Korea. Iran's program is some years off, and there are certainly things we can do to counter whatever threat it might eventually present other than building a missile defense system. And North Korea has frozen its missile flight test program at least through 2003, although they've recently suggested that if the United States abrogates the ABM treaty and employs missile defenses they'll probably resume testing.

Even if the threat were real, I think missile defenses are the wrong way to go about resolving it. I don't think building something that forces us to wait until a missile is launched is the most effective means of defending ourselves. We really can have no idea whether they will work. No matter how much money we spend on them, no matter how many tests the military conducts . . .

DJ: And cheats on . . .

SS: . . . we'll never be able to test it under real world conditions. We'll just have to cross our fingers. That's not really a rational approach.

It would be far easier and less expensive to eliminate the threat on the ground now through some sort of arms control or arms reduction agreement.

Russia provides an example of a more effective means of reducing the threat of nuclear attack. Over the last ten years the U.S. has spent about $5 billion working with Russia on the Cooperative Threat Reduction Program. This is a fraction of what's been spent on missile defenses, yet we've helped them eliminate over fifty-five hundred warheads, hundreds of ballistic missiles, and dozens of ballistic missile submarines; we've cut up bombers, and we've sealed up test holes. All of that means that those weapons and those systems will never bother anybody again.

The discourse over missile defense has by this time become something of a theological debate. The people promoting it aren't really interested in facts. They're interested in getting something out there because they truly believe it will work. Part of me would like to see all of this money spent, so they'll finally realize that in fact it *won't* work. But the part of me that pays taxes doesn't want the money spent, because so much has already been wasted.

But the real issue surrounding missile defense systems—beyond the dubious technical feasibility and beyond the exorbitant cost—is this: will we be better off with such a system than without it? I'm not convinced we will, because I think it will end up triggering regional arms races which could very easily get out of hand. First of all, I'm not convinced that countries are going to build ballistic missiles in order to attack us. But if they *are*, and they see that U.S. missile defense systems might actually work, they're not going to just throw up their hands and say, "Oh, well, we tried it. We give up. You can be the global hegemon." They'll find some other means to threaten, in ways the ballistic missile defense systems won't do anything about, like bombs on aircrafts, bombs on ships, bombs on cruise missiles, bombs covertly assembled in the United States and trucked to their targets, bombs carried overland in backpacks. We could have the world's best ballistic missile defense system that works perfectly one hundred percent of the time, and still be threatened.

The notion that American children would be able to sleep safe in their beds at night if only we had a missile defense is complete nonsense, because there are many ways that countries which might want to threaten us would be able to do so, without, by the way, using a system that has a return address stamped on it. If you think about the times the United States or its overseas troops or properties have been threatened over the past decade, it's never been with a ballistic missile. It was somebody ramming a ship into the USS Cole, it was with truck bombs that attacked U.S. embassies in Kenya and Tanzania, and earlier, in the 1980s, in Lebanon. It was the World Trade Center bombing. It was Timothy McVeigh and the Oklahoma City Bombing.

If we spend tens or hundreds of billions of dollars to deal with the most remote threat, we're going to have comparatively less money to spend on other programs. But we haven't had the debate over that yet, because the folks that are plowing ahead with this program are convinced that it is right, and won't brook dissent.

DJ: What is the relationship between extreme military spending and economic insecurity?

SS: We have a very good example of what can happen if you spend too much money on the military and too little of it on people and your economic infrastructure. It's called the Soviet Union. It doesn't exist anymore. And one of the reasons it doesn't exist is that it spent far too much of its national treasure on things military and too little of it building up the kind of infrastructure necessary to have a viable country, a viable society. They're still struggling with that today. I don't think we're in line to be the next Soviet Union, but there is that example which I think we should heed.

There are basic questions we need to ask ourselves: will we be better off with more MX missiles, or more schools to educate our children? Are we going to be better off with more aircraft carriers and stealth bombers, or with better hospitals and better health care? I could go on and on.

While we are spending less on nuclear weapons today than we were at the height of the Cold War—$35 billion a year now, down from an average of $98 billion then—we're still spending an awful lot.

DJ: Thirty-five billion could fund a lot of habitat restoration, or schools, or health care.

SS: Even George Bush, when he had a briefing a couple of months ago about the nuclear arsenal, came away amazed that we had so many nuclear weapons. He said, "I had no idea we have so many. What are they all for?"

DJ: Who benefits from all of this?

SS: Certainly the people managing the programs within the government. And just as certainly members of Congress who deliver jobs to their constituents. Norm Dicks, for example, from the Seattle area, pushed hard for more Stealth Bombers because they happened to be built in his district. While that might help him get reelected, it's not necessarily good for the country. Of course those sorts of pork barrel appropriations are nothing new. But there are two new things about them. The first is the ability in the Cold War and then today to justify them on the basis of national security, yet to cloak them in secrecy: "I can't tell you too much about this program, or what it's going to cost, but it's absolutely vital for our national security, and by the way will employ lots of people in my district." The second thing that's new is that pork-barrel projects used to be things that actually benefited people, like bridges, roads, schools and so on.

DJ: What do you want people to do with all of this information?

SS: Stand up, speak as citizens, and make certain that the government cannot ignore your voice. The current state of affairs can only exist as long as the public lets it. The government operates with the consent of the governed, and unless and until people rise up en masse like they did in the 1950s and 1960s with regard to nuclear testing and fallout, and then in the 1980s with regard to what the Reagan administration was doing with the nuclear weapons program, until they send the message to their elected representatives and to the news media that they are not willing to support nuclear weapons, nothing is going to change.

If people are dissatisfied with nuclear weapons for whatever reason—they think they're too expensive or too dangerous, or too much is being kept secret from them—they need to let people know that, and not assume somebody else will do it for them. That assumption is how you wind up with the kind of government we have today.

I would like for people to think about what it means to base our security on the threat to annihilate entire regions of the globe. I would like for them to think about what it means to have a fleet of Trident submarines, with each one capable of killing something on the order of fifty million people. Right now.

If you think that the existence of these submarines is best for you, and for everyone else, then you probably don't need to do anything. But if you disagree, and most of the people in this country do, then you might consider beginning to talk about it. Because the government will certainly continue attempting to keep these programs secret. If the programs were truly justifiable, and sound, they ought to be able to stand up to public scrutiny, but time and again they simply cannot.

You asked earlier why Americans should care about nuclear weapons. I have a question for you in return: given the stakes—both environmental and economic—why do you think so few Americans *do* care deeply about them?

I was just looking at some numbers that came in from a Harris poll. The question was: "Have you seen, heard, or read anything recently about the missile defense system that the Pentagon has been developing for testing, or not?" Fifty percent of the respondents had never heard of it. I don't think there is any comparison between the level of attention—and the attention span—surrounding these issues today as opposed to that during the Cold War. Particularly in the 1950s and 1960s, people paid much closer attention, because it was literally a matter of life and death. People don't have that sense anymore, because President Clinton and now President Bush are telling them there's nothing to worry about. The media implicitly tell them there's nothing to worry about; it's not in the news anymore, it's not really even in the movies, so what's the big deal? Nobody's rattling sabers at each other. But the weapons are still there, just hidden behind a curtain, and so we pretend they're not there at all.

The Cold War is over. It's time that the weapons, the threats, the policies changed. And there are no plans at present to change any of that. It would be wrong to think that we can go about our lives without having to worry about this anymore, just because we're not hearing about it from our elected representatives or the news media. And whether or not you think nuclear weapons are a threat, the fact is that we're still spending thirty-five billion tax dollars a year on nuclear weapons and weapons related programs. That's money that cannot be spent on other things that people have said are more important to them, like health care, education, and protecting the environment. Every decision to spend money on nuclear weapons is a *de facto* decision not to spend money on something else. As the economy slows, and as we start to tighten our belts, I think we need to look at paring away those expenses—and those entire parts of our military and economic systems—that do not benefit us.

ALFRED McCOY

Interview conducted on
April 21, 2002, at his
office in Madison, Wisconsin.

The debate over illegal drugs in the U.S. has long focused on legalization versus increased prosecution, treatment versus harsher sentences. But what's been missing on both sides of the debate is a meaningful understanding of the history and politics behind drug production and prohibition. What is the relationship, for example, between the Cold War and skyrocketing drug use in the U.S. and Europe? And why is it that, in the nearly one hundred years since the U.S. passed its first anti-drug law, the global traffic in drugs has grown astronomically?

Alfred McCoy, author of *The Politics of Heroin: CIA Complicity in the Global Drug Trade* (Lawrence Hill Books), has literally written the book on the complex relationship among drugs, prohibition, and power. Now in its third edition, the book got its start in 1970, when McCoy's editor at Harper & Row suggested he write about the explosion of heroin use among American soldiers in Vietnam. At the outset, McCoy met General Maurice Belleux, former chief of French Intelligence for Indochina, who revealed to him that the CIA, like its French predecessor, was involved in the opium trade. When beat poet and antiwar activist Allen Ginsberg heard what McCoy was writing about, he sent years' worth of unpublished dispatches from *Time-Life* correspondents—lifted from the magazine publisher's files—documenting the involvement of U.S. allies in drug trafficking. Then came the Vietnam veterans' stories of CIA helicopters transporting opium in Laos and truck convoys carrying opium down the Ho Chi Minh trail, destined for American troops in South Vietnam. That's when the death threats began.

Since then McCoy's life has been threatened many times. While he was doing research in Laos in 1971, members of the CIA's secret army ambushed and shot at him and his colleagues. But he persevered, going from the Hmong villages in the Laotian highlands, to the neon bars of Saigon, to the homes of the region's major drug lords. Everywhere he went, he asked about the history of the drug trade in the region, starting in the past, when the trade was legal, and working his way up to the present. His strategy worked.

Despite the CIA's attempts to suppress it, *The Politics of Heroin in Southeast Asia* (Harper & Row) came out in 1972. McCoy revised the book in 1991, shortening the title and including the story of the CIA's involvement in Afghanistan and that country's subsequent increase in opium production. For the 1991 edition, McCoy wrote, "Over the past twenty years, the CIA has moved from local transport of raw opium in the remote mountains of Laos to apparent complicity in the bulk transport of pure cocaine directly into the United States." He could now point to a pattern of how, over and over, "America's drug epidemics have been fueled by narcotics supplied from areas of major CIA operations, while periods of reduced heroin use coincide with the absence of CIA activity."

Controversy continues to follow McCoy. A few days before I interviewed him at his office at the University of Wisconsin in Madison, a crowd of protesters had gathered outside his building. The town of Madison had turned down a request by its Hmong community to name a park after General Vang Pao, a leader in the CIA's secret army during the Vietnam War. One of the reasons the city gave for its refusal was McCoy's account of Pao's involvement in the opium trade and his disregard for the lives of the Hmong people who fought under him on behalf of the CIA. The protesters included veterans of Pao's army. McCoy said he had met some of them before. In fact, Pao's troops were the ones who had ambushed him in Laos years ago.

In addition to writing *The Politics of Heroin*, McCoy has spent years investigating the drug trade in Australia and written and edited other books on drug trafficking, Southeast Asia, and the Philippines. Later he worked as a consultant and commentator on television and film documentaries about the global drug trade. Since then he has written the important books *A Question of Torture: CIA Interrogation, from the Cold War to the War on Terror* (Metropolitan

Books) and *Policing America's Empire: The United States, the Philippines, and the Rise of the Surveillance State* (University of Wisconsin Press).

Derrick Jensen: What do politics and heroin have to do with each other?

Alfred McCoy: Narcotics and addiction are not simply products of individual social deviance or weakness. Narcotics are a major global commodity, and commodities are the building blocks of modern life. They shape our culture. They shape our politics. Whether we encourage trade in a particular commodity or attempt to prohibit it, both acts are intensely political.

DJ: Different drugs seem to go in and out of favor. Why is heroin so significant?

AM: The global narcotics trade over the last three centuries has generally been in heroin's natural source, opium, the most venerable of drugs. Opium's original home was the eastern Mediterranean, but by the eighth century, it had spread, both in cultivation and trade, across the whole of Asia. Still, for most of its history, opium remained in limited production with very limited use. It didn't become a major commodity until the nineteenth century, when consumption rose dramatically in both Asia and the West. China, which was plagued by political and cultural turmoil at that time, appeared to have an almost limitless appetite for opium. And there was a tremendous rise in opium's use in patent medicines both in the United Kingdom and the United States.

In the late nineteenth century, the European pharmaceutical industry discovered diacetylmorphine, a chemical compound created by bonding morphine from the opium poppy with a common industrial chemical, acetic anhydride. In 1898, the Bayer Corporation launched diacetylmorphine as a cure for infant respiratory ailments, giving it the short, snappy trade name heroin. (A year later Bayer came up with an analgesic that it felt was also ideal for children's respiratory ailments, and it gave that one the short, snappy trade name aspirin.) Heroin was widely used and abused. Historian David Musto has estimated that there were three hundred thousand American opium and heroin addicts in 1900—primarily women, who were banned from barrooms and confined to a nurturing role, making this highly addictive drug marketed as a treatment for children's ailments a natural for them. You can find an evocative and very accurate depiction of this problem in Eugene O'Neill's classic play *Long Day's Journey into Night*, about his own mother's addiction.

Meanwhile, in China, the government did a survey in 1906 and found that 13.5 percent of the population of China was addicted to opium. Today, the highest level of narcotics addiction in the world, according to the United Nations, is Iran, at about 3.5 percent.

DJ: What is it in the U.S.?

AM: About 0.7 percent. The 13.5 percent figure was so astronomical that it became an international scandal and sparked a global movement for opium prohibition. This later merged ideologically and politically with the larger temperance movement in Europe, the United States, and the English-speaking colonies.

When the U.S. conquered and occupied the Philippines in 1898, it acquired, along with seven thousand islands and 6 million Filipinos, a state opium monopoly. In reaction to moral opposition among Protestant churches, the U.S. made the consumption of opium illegal in the Philippines in 1908. That eventually led to the Harrison Anti-Narcotics Act of 1914, the first of our anti-drug laws.

Since World War II, the United Nations has passed a succession of major conventions on drugs, moving from voluntary compliance and registration to international law enforcement. The interweaving of global conventions and treaties with domestic legislation has created a very powerful worldwide prohibition regime.

If we look back at the history of this regime, we find that international global commerce in illegal drugs has actually flourished during its existence. In 1998, the UN conservatively estimated international drug trafficking at $400 billion a year, equivalent to 8 percent of all world trade—larger than steel, automobiles, or textiles. So the international trade in illicit drugs is larger than the trade in one of the fundamentals of life: clothing.

DJ: Didn't we miss an opportunity at the end of World War II to drastically reduce the traffic in illegal drugs?

AM: There was a confluence of factors in the late 1940s that might have led to a substantial reduction, or even elimination, of the global traffic in illicit drugs. The first factor was the increased effectiveness of the global prohibition regime. The second was the worldwide disruption of all trade and the rigid security imposed upon ports around the globe to stop sabotage, espionage, and the like. The third factor was the Communists' rise to power in China in 1949, soon after which they ran the world's most successful opium-eradication campaign, eliminating mass narcotics addiction in the space of about five years.

We'll never know what might have transpired if Western intelligence agencies hadn't used the power of the underground drug economy and its criminal syndicates to fight communism. If the CIA hadn't existed, would we have the levels of addiction we see today? I can't say. But I can say that covert operations played a significant role in the expansion of drug trafficking after World War II.

Beginning in the late 1940s, the Iron Curtain came crashing down along the southern border of the Soviet Union and the People's Republic of China. This was also the Asian opium zone, a mountain rim that stretches five thousand miles, from Turkey to Thailand. Over a period of forty years, from 1950 to 1990, the CIA fought three major covert wars—not just espionage, but actual secret wars—along this rugged southern frontier, the soft underbelly of communism. This included Burma, during the 1950s; Laos, from 1964 to 1974; and Afghanistan, where the CIA backed the *mujaheddin* guerillas against the Soviet occupation from 1979 to 1992.

These were long wars. The U.S. was involved in World War I for less than two years and World War II for four. These covert wars lasted ten to and twelve years and in some cases involved massive military operations. The largest bombing campaign in history was the U.S. air operation in Laos in support of the CIA's secret war there.

These wars were generally fought at the margins of states that didn't support our efforts, in ethnic minority-populated areas where the main cash crop was opium. The CIA found out that, to fight covert wars in such remote regions, it had to ally itself with local warlords, who in turn used the CIA's protection and logistics expertise to transform themselves into drug lords.

At the start of each of these wars, the opium production was localized. Very quickly, however, both the scale and scope of the traffic expanded in order to fund the wars. By the time the operations were over, the regions were wastelands in which only the poppy would flower. Because these wars were conducted outside conventional diplomacy and beyond Congressional oversight, there were no postwar settlements, no treaties or reconstruction. Officially, they *never happened*. In the absence of any cleanup, expanded drug trafficking served as an ad hoc form of reconstruction.

In 1958, authorities in northeastern Burma estimated annual local opium production to be about eighteen tons. By 1970 it was three hundred tons. The net result of the CIA's covert operation was that northeastern Burma went from localized opium trade to being the heart of the global heroin market. Laos went from similarly limited production to being the world's number-three opium producer today.

The purest case of transformation, though, was Afghanistan. At the time we got involved in Afghanistan, its annual opium production was no more than two hundred tons, with trade limited to the central Asian region, particularly Iran. There was no heroin production, and no international trafficking. From 1981 to 1991, opium production in Afghanistan grew to two thousand tons—a tenfold increase. Just two years into the secret war, Afghanistan, in concert with western Pakistan, had become the world's largest heroin producer, supplying, according to the U.S. Attorney General, 60 percent of the heroin in the U.S. and about 80 percent of Europe's heroin. Today the world's three leading producers of illicit opium are Afghanistan, Burma (now Myanmar), and Laos—all sites of former CIA covert wars that ran a decade or more.

DJ: How is it in the CIA's interest to do this?

AM: Basically, when the Agency mounts a covert operation, a handful of operatives form an alliance with one or more local warlords. The warlords raise an army to fight the CIA's battle, and the agents provide their warlord allies with arms, supplies, funds, food, and political support. They do this not only to make that tribal leader more militarily effective, but also so he'll increase his power over his tribe and draw more recruits who will fight in a more determined and committed way.

Now, along this southern frontier of Communist territory, the sole cash crop is opium. So as the tribal warlord grows in power, he takes over the opium trade, and thus takes over the household economy of every farming family. It's in the CIA's interest to tolerate opium traffic because it increases the political power of the Agency's chosen ally and makes the CIA's covert army more effective.

Moreover, as the fighting gets going and the men are drawn into the war, the male labor pool drops. Opium harvesting is, in many highland cultures, women's work. The men may clear land and plant the seed, but the women harvest, and a poppy field can stay in production in Southeast Asia for as long as a decade. This means the women are productively employed in producing a high-income cash crop, which cuts down the CIA's cost of supporting its tribal allies.

DJ: Where is international law enforcement while all this is going on?

AM: Crucially, these covert war zones become enforcement-free zones into which international and local law enforcement don't venture. The classic case of this was Afghanistan in the 1980s. During that decade, when literally hundreds of heroin kitchens lined the Afghan-Pakistani border, the U.S. Drug Enforcement Administration had a detachment of seventeen officers in the Pakistani capital of Islamabad. These officers conducted no investigations and made no seizures or arrests. They stayed entirely out of the northwest frontier province of Pakistan, where the heroin industry was sited, because the traffickers were our covert allies.

DJ: Hasn't the CIA also allowed its airplanes to be used for transporting illegal drugs?

AM: I know of one particular case of that, in Laos. Let me give you some background: during the Cold War, the Soviet Union and the United States went to the brink over Laos before negotiating a treaty in 1962 in which both sides agreed to remove all combat forces from the country. Two or three years later, the Vietnam War heated up, and suddenly the North Vietnamese were sending troops and supplies from the panhandle of North Vietnam, down through southern Laos, and into South Vietnam: the infamous Ho Chi Minh Trail. Unless the U.S. could cut off that supply route, we had no hope of winning our war of attrition in South Vietnam. Suddenly we had to be involved in a country where we could not be involved. That led to the secret war in Laos, in which the CIA turned the Hmong tribesmen into an army. The Hmong, who were the main opium growers in the region, lived on highland ridges above three thousand feet. With road travel dangerous to impossible during the war, their villages were linked together by a network of two hundred dirt landing strips accessed by a CIA airline called Air America.

In 1971, when I was doing research for *The Politics of Heroin*, I hiked into Hmong villages in northern Laos at the western edge of the Plain of Jars region. I went from house to house in the two villages where I was able to conduct my survey, and the picture was pretty clear. Farmers were harvesting about five to ten kilos of opium each. At the end of harvest season, they took the pungent raw opium, wrapped in banana leaves, down to the landing strip—and the farmers' stories were absolutely consistent on this score—where an Air America helicopter landed. Hmong officers in the CIA's secret army got out, paid the tribesmen cash for their opium, loaded it onto the helicopters, and flew away in the direction of the CIA's secret base at Long Tieng.

Up until the mid-sixties, opium buyers would lead strings of packhorses into Hmong villages to purchase opium, or the farmers would hike down to local markets and sell it there. But as the communist guerillas and the North Vietnamese forces began sweeping through these valleys, all transportation beneath the ridges was disrupted. Air America was the only way in and out of the Hmong villages. If they were going to market their opium, it was going to be through Air America: there was no alternative. And the opium trade was one of the pillars of economic survival for these people.

The use of Air America also increased the power of the warlords. Before the CIA's aircraft would fly in to pick up opium, there had to be an authorization from the secret army's commanders. And because of growing casualties as the secret war spread, rice production crashed. The villages were no longer self-sufficient in rice, so Air America would fly over and drop bags of rice. The delivery of relief rice into villages, and the transport of opium out of them, gave the Hmong warlords a stranglehold on the population.

As this war ground on, the tremendous casualties threatened the tribe with generational extinction of young males. In 1971 a U.S. Air Force report said that the oldest males in many Hmong families were ten years old.

DJ: So why did the Hmong keep fighting for the CIA?

AM: Most didn't want to. When I went into those villages to do my survey, it was at a particularly tense time, because the CIA's secret army had put out a call for fourteen-year-olds. The village elders had gotten together and said, "No. We've lost everybody above this age, and if we start handing over the fourteen-year-olds, then the thirteen-year-olds and all the rest are going to follow, and who will marry the women and produce the next generation? We're going to die. We can't do this."

When this village refused to send its young males to the slaughter, its rice was cut off. And they were hungry. That was actually the reason I was able to do my research: I made a deal with the village leader.

Now, this was a nonliterate person—not illiterate, but nonliterate, because the Hmong had an oral culture. When I told him I wanted to know about opium, he said, "Can you get an article in a newspaper in Washington, D.C., saying that we gave our sons to fight in the CIA's secret war, and part of the deal was that we would get rice?"

I said I knew a correspondent for *The Washington Post*, but I couldn't guarantee anything.

He told me I could ask anybody I wanted about the opium, and he'd send an escort with me, because there was a lot of guerrilla activity in the area.

So I talked to the people in his village, asking: How much opium do you produce? What do you do at harvest time? Where do you take it? How much do you get for it?

We later found out that a Hmong captain was radioing reports to the command of the CIA's secret army about the questions we were asking. As we made our way to the next village to continue our survey, some soldiers in warlord Vang Pao's army ambushed us and tried to kill us.

When we got back to the Laotian capital of Vientiane, I went to see the head of the U.S. Agency for International Development (USAID), Charlie Mann, who had ambassadorial rank. I complained both that CIA's militia had tried to kill us, and that the rice, which was supposed to be humanitarian relief, had been cut off. Then I spoke to the *Washington Post* correspondent. Within days, a small article appeared in the back pages of *The Washington Post*. As that nonliterate Hmong leader had expected, Air America's C-130 cargo planes bombarded his village with rice from USAID.

But that's how that system operated: control over the opium and rice amplified the warlord's power and allowed him to extract soldiers, in this case boy soldiers, for slaughter in the CIA's secret war.

DJ: What happened to all the opium? Where was it sold?

AM: Most of it was turned into heroin for sale to U.S. soldiers. The secret war in Laos introduced heroin-refining technology into the region. In 1969 and 1970, the armies that fought alongside the CIA's secret army in Laos built a complex of seven heroin refineries at the heart of the Golden Triangle, where Burma, Thailand, and Laos converge. Let me make this clear: all the laboratories were built by current or former covert allies of the United States. And they began producing high-grade heroin for shipment to South Vietnam. The local Asian addicts were opium smokers, which means the heroin was targeted purely at American troops. We know from a later White House survey that, by 1971, 34 percent of all U.S. combat forces in South Vietnam were using heroin. That means there were something like eighty thousand heroin addicts in the U.S. Army at a point when there were only about seventy thousand addicts in the entire United States.

DJ: You've said that the CIA's secret war in Laos had a broader legacy than just increased opium production.

AM: Yes, it changed the way we fight wars. Up until the Laos operation, conventional military wisdom said that only infantry could take and hold ground; air power could merely provide tactical support for infantry and destroy strategic targets. We couldn't send troops into Laos, though, without violating our treaty with the Soviet Union. So we dropped 2.1 million tons of bombs on Laos—roughly equal to the tonnage we dropped in the whole of World War II. And we learned that if you bomb intensively and without restraint, you can actually use aerial bombardment as a means to take and hold ground. We used this strategy successfully in Bosnia, where we sent in very few combat forces, and even more successfully in Kosovo.

The problem with this strategy is that it produces serious violations of international law. When the international community saw our destructive use of air power in the Vietnam War, it became concerned about the enormous "collateral damage" the bombing caused. As the Vietnam War was winding down, the international community negotiated Protocol One of the Geneva Convention, which outlawed military attacks on civilians. They went even further and created the International Criminal Court to try those who violated the laws of the convention. Although the United States was one of the prime movers in creating the Geneva Convention in 1949, President Reagan sent the treaty for Protocol One to the Senate with the recommendation that it be rejected, and it was.

On April 4, 2002, the world had a ceremony to celebrate the establishment of the International Criminal Court. The U.S. did not send representatives. We are proposing to lead this "new world order" governed by the rule of law, yet because we're increasingly wedded to air power and its broad use against both civilian and military targets, we are at odds with the international laws the rest of the world supports. As we move into the twenty-first century, these covert wars have left a very problematic legacy for the conduct of U.S. foreign policy.

DJ: Afghanistan is the most recent covert war, and the one most directly related to current events. How did it come about?

AM: In a very similar fashion to the war in Laos. Starting in 1979, the Carter administration—and later the Reagan White House—gave executive orders to the CIA to arm and supply the Afghan resistance to the Soviet occupation of Afghanistan. The only difference is that this was an international conflict, not just a U.S. operation. The Saudis, for example, heavily supported the Afghan rebels, as did the Europeans.

Still, from 1979 to 1992 the CIA spent approximately $3 billion on this secret war, routing most of the money through Pakistan's Inter-Services Intelligence, or ISI. The result was a tenfold expansion of opium production inside Afghanistan, and growth in trade from localized opium distribution to large scale heroin refining for the international market. In a pattern we see time and again, the tribal warlords inside Afghanistan were transformed into powerful drug lords.

After investing $3 billion in Afghanistan's destruction, the United States simply walked away at the end of the operation, leaving behind a wasted society. Afghanistan was our longest covert war, and in many ways the most severely devastated of our covert battlegrounds. The fighting left behind a million dead, 4.5 million refugees, and an estimated 10 million landmines—not to mention a ruined economy and a ravaged government. After the Soviets were defeated, the warlords we had created and armed began fighting among themselves for power, adding to the devastation.

As Afghanistan's postwar problems multiplied, opium offered the simplest solution. In the devastated economy, there was astronomical unemployment. Opium is very labor intensive; it takes nine times as much labor to harvest a hectare of opium than it does a hectare of wheat. So it put people to work.

Opium also commands a high international price, which meant the impoverished farmers could finance the rehabilitation of their farms and communities. Another obstacle to reconstruction was that international agricultural commodities are traded through a very complex diplomacy; having no recognized government, Afghanistan didn't have the capacity for such diplomacy. As an illicit commodity, however, opium could easily pass across every border in the world. And then there were the periodic droughts: opium uses about half the water of food crops. So from every perspective, opium was the ideal solution to Afghanistan's postwar problems.

Under conditions of civil war in Afghanistan, from 1992 to 1996, opium production continued to climb upward. When the Taliban took power in Kabul in 1996, only three countries in the world recognized the new government, and Afghanistan remained detached from the international economy. The Taliban quickly realized what the warlords they'd superseded had known: the only way to operate a state economy "off the grid" was through narcotics. So they not only continued to tolerate the drug traffic; they imposed a kind of rough order that increased the commerce and made it more efficient. Opium production inside Afghanistan doubled. By 1999, they were producing an extraordinary forty-six hundred tons of opium a year—enough to supply 75 percent of the world's heroin users.

Afghanistan had become the first nation in history whose economy was built predominantly upon opium. The drug trade accounted for most government revenue and all foreign exchange. It also absorbed most of the country's merchant capital and much of its water and prime arable land. And, above all, opium provided employment for about 25 percent of the adult males, which means 25 percent of the workforce, because under the Taliban women couldn't work.

By 2000, though, the Taliban had become desperate for international recognition. Throughout their brief rule, they had more or less offered the UN a deal, saying indirectly, "We'll eradicate opium if you'll give us diplomatic recognition." Then, in July 2000, the Taliban issued an opium ban and, with characteristic ruthlessness, eradicated 99 percent of the opium crop in their territory, which was most of the country. Afghanistan's opium production crashed from forty-six hundred tons to around a hundred tons. The Taliban then sent a delegation to the UN, accusing the Northern Alliance, which still held an enclave in the northeast, of being drug lords, heroin traffickers, and thugs, and said, "We've eradicated opium. Give us diplomatic recognition." The UN refused.

So when the U.S. invaded Afghanistan after September 11, 2001, we were invading a country that had been through a decade of covert war, then a decade of civil war, and finally an act of economic suicide. By the time we attacked, there was nothing left except the Taliban's rather weak, badly led army of forty thousand men. Refugees had been flowing out of Afghanistan for more than a year, not just because of drought, but because the Taliban had destroyed the country's largest source of employment and only export. Once we invaded, the society quickly collapsed.

When planning the Afghan War, the United States realized that the only allies we had were the Northern Alliance: the same warlords we had armed back in the 1980s, and who in the 1990s had operated pretty much as independent drug lords. The Northern Alliance controlled the one territory inside Afghanistan that hadn't banned drugs, and they were still very large opium producers and heroin smugglers. More important, they had huge stockpiles of opium left over from the 1999 bumper crop, which the world market simply hadn't been able to absorb: about 60 percent of the opium had been held back after the harvest. The Northern Alliance now transformed much of that opium into heroin and smuggled it into Europe and Russia.

These are the forces with which the U.S. allied itself to fight the Taliban, and the forces we have since installed in power in Afghanistan. The wisdom of that decision has proven dubious, even militarily speaking. During the bungled Tora Bora operation, when it looked as if the U.S. had Osama bin Laden and most of al-Qaeda cornered in caves, one of those warlords, Hazarat Ali, controlled the territory between the caves and the Pakistani border. With a warlord's eye for business, he sold al-Qaeda "Get Out of Afghanistan Alive" cards for a bargain price of about five thousand dollars a head.

As we speak, there's a big new crop of opium pushing its way out of the soil across Afghanistan. It's going to be politically very embarrassing for the U.S. when our invasion and liberation of Afghanistan floods Europe with unprecedented quantities of heroin.

DJ: How does all of this relate to the drug war in the United States?

AM: Since 1971, under President Nixon, we've spent approximately $150 billion to fight five "drug wars." That's not quite half the cost of the Vietnam War. And that doesn't include state and local costs for prosecution and incarceration. The cost of building and operating prisons for nonviolent drug offenders is enormous.

The expanded drug war that has been fought since the mid-eighties, primarily with longer jail sentences, has created an enormous prison population and done incredible damage to racial harmony in this society. From 1930 to 1980, American society had, on average, a hundred prisoners per hundred thousand people. After Reagan's drug war started in the 1980s, that grew to four hundred per hundred thousand. We're now well above six hundred per hundred thousand.

The Sentencing Project has found that about a third of African American males between the ages of eighteen and thirty are either on parole, in prison, or under indictment. And the lion's share of them are incarcerated for possession or petty sale of narcotics. When these African American men emerge from prison, they're stripped of their civil rights. In many states, they can't vote. This represents the criminalization and the political disenfranchisement of an entire community. Unless we turn it off, this doomsday machine will keep sweeping the streets for drug users, filling the prisons, and adding to these enormous social costs.

DJ: I'm not as familiar with Nixon's drug war. How was it fought?

AM: From the late 1940s to the early 1970s, the infamous French Connection was the source of about 80 percent of America's heroin supply. Here's how it worked: Turkey had farmers producing opium to sell to licensed pharmaceutical companies for use in making morphine. These farmers routinely produced more than their quota, shipping their bootleg opium down to Lebanon, where it was refined into morphine and shipped to France. There, the Corsican syndicates, protected by French Intelligence and the Gaullist government, operated a complex of labs that transformed the morphine into heroin. They shipped it to Montreal, Canada, where the Cotroni Mafia family shipped it down to New York for distribution across the Eastern Seaboard.

Because the farmers in Turkey were all licensed for legal pharmaceutical production, the Turkish government knew who they all were. At Nixon's demand, the Turks simply went out and eradicated opium. The U.S. provided around $30 million to help the farmers make the transition to other crops. We then leaned on the French, who of course knew exactly who the traffickers were, because they all belonged to a paramilitary organization called the Civic Action Service that actually provided state security for the Gaullist regime. The French police closed down the heroin labs, and the French Connection was destroyed in a matter of months. Nixon scored a total victory.

But every victory in the drug war lays the groundwork for a later defeat. Demand for heroin was still high, and there was now a shortfall in supply, so the international price went up, creating a strong incentive for a boom in production in Southeast Asia. To add to this, the Vietnam War was over, the last of the GIs were gone, and Southeast Asia's opium producers had a surplus. Suddenly the U.S. began getting large shipments of heroin from Southeast Asia.

So Nixon fought and won another battle in his drug war. He sent thirty Drug Enforcement Agency agents to Bangkok, where they did a very effective job of seizing heroin bound for the United States, imposing a kind of informal customs duty on it. The Southeast Asian traffickers simply turned around and exported to Europe, which had been virtually drug free for decades. You see, the French syndicates had an agreement with the Gaullist government: they could manufacture heroin, but they couldn't sell it in France. With the French Connection out of the picture, the Southeast Asian syndicates were free to flood Europe with heroin. By the end of the 1970s, Europe had more heroin addicts than the United States.

Each time we bring the blunt baton of law enforcement down upon this illicit global market, we create an increase in price, which in turn stimulates production and geographical proliferation. Intervention at the level of trafficking only forces drug lords to create ever more complex smuggling networks. The net result of these drug wars is that there has been a six-fold increase in global opium production since they began.

It's the same with cocaine in South America. In the fifteen years we've been fighting a drug war in the Andes, cocaine production in the region has doubled. During the 1990s, the pursuit of the drug war in Peru brought the CIA into alliance with Vladimiro Montesinos, the head of state security under the Fujimori dictatorship. Today, he is in prison for corruption, and his overseas bank accounts hold a quarter of a billion dollars in drug money. He single-handedly corrupted Peruvian democracy. And for each hectare of cocoa that was taken out in Peru, one was added in Colombia. Now we're applying pressure on Colombia, and Peruvian production is coming back up. And of course our covert involvement in the politics of these nations damages our relationship with them over the long term.

The UN has the idea, and the United States as well, that because narcotics production is concentrated in a few limited areas, we can make a knockout blow and end this drug problem once and for all. The U.S. favors "aerial defoliation." The UN favors crop substitution. But they both share a belief that they can, after nearly a century of effort, finally eradicate the narcotics trade. And it's possible, in theory—and sometimes in reality—to apply enough coercive force to extirpate an illegal commodity from a community. But as we've seen, in an age of illicit global commodities and transnational organized crime, the traffic just slips sideways into other areas, to infinity.

Let's just assume, however, that the U.S. and UN were somehow able to succeed. Let us imagine that in this new world order the prohibition regime is finally able to eliminate opium production.

This would put in place a situation mirroring Nixon's second victory. When we disrupted the flow of heroin from Southeast Asia to America, Mexican syndicates began producing large quantities of cannabis for shipment to the United States. In 1975, the Ford administration began a massive marijuana eradication effort in Mexico and sealed the border. The result was that much of the marijuana production shifted south to Colombia, laying the economic foundation for the drug cartels that a decade later switched to cocaine production.

The most dramatic change in the last decade has been the global rise of synthetic drugs, especially amphetamine-type substances (ATS). Currently, there are about 14 million opiate abusers in the world, and about the same number of coca abusers. There are 30 million ATS abusers. It's as big as opium and cocaine combined. One of the things about ATS is that the labs are sited very close to consumer areas, so interdiction is essentially impossible.

We've gone from the simple, straight-line network of the French Connection to an infinitely complex global system that resists intervention. The drug war isn't simply failing; it's counterproductive. Prohibition stimulates production. Any economics expert could tell you that. If you told the Federal Reserve that adjusting interest rates has no impact on the American economy, they would laugh at you. That's the *point* of adjusting interest rates. That's the *point* of market intervention. Yet all these law enforcement agencies—from the DEA to state police—think they can intervene in the illicit drug market without affecting trade. There is no "immaculate intervention." Intervention, particularly unwitting intervention, only makes the problem worse.

DJ: Where does all of this leave us concerning the war on drugs?

AM: I think prohibition is going to be substantially revised in the years to come, though not completely discarded. Legalization isn't politically possible in the short term—or even the medium term—given that prohibition is embedded in so many state and federal laws, not to mention international treaties. There's no political will to unravel all of that at this point.

The debate has now moved from prohibition to pragmatics. We're no longer talking about whether drugs are moral or immoral. Instead, we're starting to ask: What works? What are the costs? Drugs may be illegal, but incarceration is not a rational way to treat drug abuse. We'll hear more states saying, "Let's give people treatment." I think there will be a shift toward minimizing the damage, both from drugs and from law enforcement. Within ten years, I expect we'll see no incarceration for personal possession. Part of the reason is that we can move from mass incarceration to mass treatment without changing state, national, and international drug laws. All we have to do is change sentencing.

The boom economy of the 1990s is over. We're beyond the dot-com age. Money is now real, and fiscal choices are severe. Faced with a choice between mass incarceration or better education, what will most people choose? What about a choice between more prisons for nonviolent drug offenders or prescription drug benefits for senior citizens? I think economic reality is going to force us to ask whether this drug war is working. With referenda requiring treatment instead of jail terms for first-time drug users in California, Arizona, and Nevada, we can already see the shape of things to come.

CHRISTIAN PARENTI

Interview conducted on
March 14, 2000, at his home
in San Francisco, California.

I used to teach creative writing inside a prison. That does not make me an expert on prisons.

I can, however, talk about those things I have experienced directly, such as my classes. So, though I cannot tell you the entire judicial and penal system is racist, I can tell you that nearly all of my minimum-security students have been white, and nearly all of my maximum-security students have been black, Hispanic, Asian, American Indian, or "other."

And I cannot tell you about conditions inside the Security Housing Units, but I can tell you that these windowless concrete buildings sit in the middle of a graveled dead zone, and that I have taught prisoners who have lived there in solitary confinement for up to sixteen years. (One student told me he did not see another living creature—save his guards—for years. Then one day, while he was being led in shackles to the infirmary, a dragonfly hovered next to him and followed him as he walked.)

I cannot tell you whether guards set prisoners against one another, but I can tell you of a conversation I had with a prison counselor who was trying to convince me to take a full-time job at the prison teaching remedial English. I told him it would cut too much into my writing time.

"Write when they're locked down," he said.

"And when they're not?"

"Easy," he said. "Tell Hartley that Johnson is talking shit about him, then say the same to Johnson. Next time they're on the yard, one sticks the other, and you've got instant lockdown."

He laughed as he said this.

I also cannot tell you whether a disrespect for human life pervades the prison system, but I can tell you this story: Several months ago, I arrived to teach my class and was told there would be no class that day because of an incident on the yard. "Shots were fired," a guard said.

"My God," I said. "Is everything all right?"

He assured me no one had been hurt.

I later found out nine inmates had been shot, one killed. No staff had been injured.

Christian Parenti can tell you much more than I. He is an expert on the prison system, having researched and studied it as a journalist, scholar, and student for the past decade. His first book, *Lockdown America: Police and Prisons in the Age of Crisis* (Verso Books), is an articulate critique of what he calls the "incipient American police state." We've become a country where, in some states, prison budgets exceed spending on higher learning; where companies like Starbucks, Jansport, and Microsoft use prison labor in their packaging departments; where Corrections Corporation of America, the nation's largest private prison operator, was dubbed a "theme stock for the nineties." In addition to documenting the absurd reality of modern incarceration, Parenti relates the history of the current prison buildup in accessible and engaging prose—perhaps too accessible: *Lockdown America* was banned from Angola State Penitentiary in Louisiana because it "promotes gang violence and homosexuality." The *British Independent* had a more favorable view: "In the best tradition of investigative journalism, paced like a fine novel, it carries the authority of meticulous academic research."

Born and raised in rural New England, Parenti first became interested in criminal justice while an undergraduate at the New School for Social Research in New York City. But it was the police activity he witnessed living in both New York City and San Francisco that brought home to him the central role of law enforcement and incarceration in American politics. He has three books out, plus a new edition of *Lockdown America*. I've long been a fan of his articles in the *Nation*, the *Progressive*, *In These Times*, the *Christian Science Monitor*, and *Z* magazine. He has also worked as a radio journalist in Central America, New York, and California.

Parenti and I met for this interview on a beautiful spring day at his home in the Mission District. His warm and articulate manner made me feel immediately welcome and allowed me to get right to the point: the American prison-industrial complex.

Derrick Jensen: How big is the U.S. prison system?

Christian Parenti: It's huge. Our country has only 4 percent of the world's population and 25 percent of the world's prisoners. There are about 2 million Americans in prisons and jails across the country and about 5 million more under the supervision of the criminal justice system—that is, awaiting trial or on probation or parole. China, by comparison, has a population of 1 billion, but only around three hundred thousand people in prison.

If you're black, the picture gets even grimmer. Although African Americans make up only 13 percent of the general population, they comprise 58 percent of the prison population and 74 percent of all prisoners convicted on drug charges. This country imprisons black men nine times more frequently than it does white men. According to one study, a third of all black men between the ages of twenty and twenty-nine were under some sort of criminal justice supervision in 1995. It's a form of apartheid.

Sociologist Loïc Wacqaunt calls criminal justice the latest development in an age-old project of controlling black people with force. We've gone from slavery to Jim Crow to this new color-coded "anticrime" justice system. Other people of color are also targeted: Latinos (one in eight young Hispanic men is imprisoned), some Asian-American groups, and Native Americans. Racism intervenes at every stage of the criminal-justice process: arrest, arraignment, indictment, trial, conviction, and sentencing. At each step, privilege acts to cull whites out.

When you look at probation, policing, parole, incarceration, and the courts as an integral web, you start to feel the breadth of the system, in terms of how many people work for and are controlled by it. Incarceration alone costs this country about $35 billion annually, employs more than 525,000 full-time workers (more than any Fortune 500 company except General Motors), and puts a couple of million people under intense regulation.

The system is expanding all the time. There's a new phenomenon in South Dakota, and probably elsewhere, called CHINS—Children in Need of Supervision. These are just kids who've been truant or have otherwise misbehaved, and their parents call in the state to put the kids on probation. The kids haven't been convicted of any crime, yet when some of them then violate probation, they end up in juvenile prisons called "boot camps." There's no trial, no conviction. I've heard horror stories from these camps of guards punishing teenage girls for minor infractions by tying them spread-eagle to a concrete slab and cutting off their clothes with scissors. And many of these girls have long histories of emotional, sexual, and physical abuse.

DJ: How did we get to this state of affairs?

CP: Official criminological histories generally begin in the Northeast, with the birth of American penitentiaries, but there is an alternative history that, I think, makes more sense. Yale University instructor Robert Perkinson calls slavery the real birth of American incarceration. He says the measures taken to control the black population in the South—particularly black males—are the true antecedents of modern criminal justice. For example, the anti-slave militias of the South, called "patrollers," did many of the same things cops do now: traveling assigned "beats," stopping black people, demanding to see their papers, and ransacking their homes looking for contraband, such as "excess" food that might indicate a slave was preparing to take off.

Then, after the Civil War, the "black codes" arose, and southern criminal justice as we know it was born. By the 1880s and 1890s, southern criminologists were talking about the "innate criminality" of black people. Those last twenty years of the nineteenth century also saw a huge explosion of incarceration in the South. Black people, rather than being kept as slaves, were being put into prison camps. Traditionally, southern prisons had been very small. The period after the Civil War brought the first great wave of imprisonment in American criminal justice.

The current prison buildup really began in the 1960s, because of two crises: an economic crisis and a political crisis.

DJ: Noam Chomsky has discussed the notion of the political crisis of the 1960s as a "crisis of democracy."

CP: Exactly: too *much* democracy. The 1960s brought the civil rights movement, the black power movement, the poor people's movement, the antiwar movement, and all sorts of informal rebellion. At first, the police were unable to contain this uprising, which was a big embarrassment for the U.S., because we were waging a bitter ideological struggle with the Soviets to prove that capitalism and liberal democracy were better than socialism. When the entire world saw images of Watts and Detroit going up in flames and angry black people describing in detail how they were being held down by the system, it exposed the lies in the idea that true democracy and racial progress were present in the U.S. So the federal government was very concerned about the failure of the police to contain the rebellion.

DJ: How were the cops failing?

CP: They were applying either too little repression and allowing things to get out of hand, or too much repression—cracking heads indiscriminately—and creating an international scandal and further radicalizing the movements. So in 1967, the federal government stepped in. President Lyndon Johnson proposed legislation that became the Omnibus Crime and Safe Streets Act—the first big federal anticrime bill of the type that's now so familiar.

That crime bill created the Law Enforcement Assistance Administration (LEAA), which, over the next ten years, distributed about a billion dollars a year to local police departments and created the infrastructure of modern policing: SWAT teams, helicopters, body armor, all of that. In addition to the qualitative shift, there was an increase in police numbers.

All of this happened because society was changing, resulting in major demographic and social upheaval. But there was also a political element in the police retooling, a way in which it was aimed at crushing a political enemy in addition to maintaining order. If you go back and read the *FBI Law Enforcement Bulletin* and the police industry press of the time, you'll find numerous quotes from FBI Director J. Edgar Hoover and people like Daryl Gates (later chief of the Los Angeles Police Department) about "putting down rebellion" and how the police are the "front-line troops" in what amounted to a counterinsurgency campaign.

DJ: In some ways, this wasn't new. Think of the Palmer raids after World War I, in which many radicals and socialists were thrown in jail. And all along, the police have been used to put down strikes.

CP: That's right. We need to remember that, while the police may get kittens out of trees and enhance public safety, their social control function has been at the heart of the job from the beginning, even though it's not most of what they do. In the sixties, however, law enforcement's political task came to the fore.

Funding for the LEAA plateaued in the 1970s, in large part because of pressure from the Left, but then the whole process started over in the 1980s with President Reagan's phony war on drugs. This time, it wasn't about putting down rebellion, because the movements had largely been demobilized. This time, the police were to maintain social order while Reaganomics threatened the economic fortunes of millions of working people.

The nation's economic troubles really began in the late 1960s, by which time the postwar boom had pretty much petered out. The conditions that had sustained the "golden era" of American capitalism were gone, and so were the abnormally high profit rates of that era. Big business in the U.S. faced ever-higher tax rates and wage demands. Out of this came the economic crisis of the seventies: rising unemployment simultaneous with rising wages, something that had never happened before. In part, this was due to the fact that working people still had a safety net. If you were treated poorly at your job, you could quit, get food stamps, and go to community college. Strikers in the early 1970s received welfare.

In the 1980s, Reagan dealt with all of this by cutting taxes on corporations, attacking labor, eviscerating social services, and so on. As a result, by the mid-1980s, profit rates had been restored, labor had been cowed, and the cost of maintaining the state had been shifted from business to everyone else. But this transformation created a massive new wave of poverty, and the war on drugs was a response to these newly reemerging class distinctions. It served to segregate and contain the dangerous classes.

Though the poor were not rebelling, they were still a threat. Poor people threaten the system's legitimacy in that they make the social structure appear unjust. They also pose an aesthetic threat, scaring and disturbing the moneyed classes by showing up in inconvenient places. And whether or not poor people are, at the moment, organized and rebelling, there's always the threat that they will. So, with Reaganomics, we again find massive resources being poured into policing.

DJ: Why not just help the poor?

CP: That's sometimes necessary, but, fundamentally, helping the poor means empowering labor, which means higher costs and lower profits for business. When Federal Reserve Chairman Alan Greenspan talks about a "natural rate of unemployment," he means that there has to be a class of people who are impoverished and desperate. Otherwise the working class would be able to demand more and more of the economic pie, and profits would drop.

DJ: But the unemployment rate is supposedly lower than it's been in decades.

CP: It is, but all that means is that there are a lot more shitty jobs out there. And the economic elites are worried that this booming economy will lead to inflation, which leads to "wage pressure," which is a code word for working-class power and political action.

The misleading thing about the unemployment rate is that it describes only the percentage of the population that is actively looking for work. It doesn't take into consideration discouraged workers. There are 2 to 4 million men who have dropped below the statistical radar because they are not involved in the official economy or don't have an official residence or both. Unemployment may be lower than it's been in thirty years, but the idea that less than 4 percent of the population is unemployed is a fiction.

A far more important statistic than unemployment is the poverty rate. The official poverty level for a family of four is $16,500, but there's been some discussion about raising it to $19,500. By that new figure, there are 47 million Americans living at or below the poverty level. That's an enormous population to keep locked into the bottom tier of society. Steven Spritzer, a radical criminologist, divides this population into two categories: "social dynamite" and "social junk." (I call the latter "social wreckage" because I find the term "junk" a little dehumanizing.)

Social dynamite are those members of the poor population who threaten to explode. They feel they are owed something and have the wherewithal to make political and social demands—that is, to resist in an organized or unorganized fashion. They're the angry young people who form political movements or gangs.

The social wreckage are those who accept their marginalized lot in society: the injured workers, the mentally ill, the people who've been beaten down for too long and have given up. They don't threaten rebellion, but they do pose an aesthetic threat. They include the people who mutter to themselves and push shopping carts around, the ones the hotel and tourist industries are so concerned about keeping out of downtowns because they freak out tourists. So long as they stay out of sight, nobody cares about them.

Social wreckage tend to get treated with a soft touch by the police and social services—*after* they've been driven away from the beaches, malls, and shopping areas of our theme park cities. Social dynamite receive a more aggressive and coordinated approach. It doesn't work simply to sweep them aside. They require both a defensive policy of containment and an offensive policy of direct attack. And if any members of this class should come together, their organizations must be destabilized and smashed. They must be confined to ghettos, warehoused in public schools, demonized by the media, condemned to prison, or dispatched by lethal injection or police bullets. Ultimately, they must be kept in check by force.

DJ: So far, we've been talking about policing and prisons in functionalist terms: describing why such institutions are necessary in a capitalist society to control the poor. But doesn't having so many people in prison create at least as many problems as it "solves"?

CP: Increasingly, we're seeing more layers added to the criminal justice system that are unnecessary in terms of regulating society; they're nonsensical, even from a capitalist perspective, and constitute what philosopher Herbert Marcuse called "surplus repression."

The recently passed Proposition 21 here in California is an example. Designed to target gang members and toughen California's juvenile justice system, it will cost $5 billion over the next ten years and send at least thirty-eight thousand youths to adult prisons, where many of them will be psychologically destroyed before being dumped back on the street.

Proposition 21 was redundant in terms of class and racial control. We were already sending youths to adult prisons. We already had the nation's highest youth incarceration rate. But the proposition wasn't put on the ballot to create a "useful" law. Rather, it was devised as a short-term campaign tool by our former governor, Pete Wilson. Wilson thought he had a chance at the Republican presidential nomination and wanted to create something that would give him a national profile and help turn out conservative voters for California's March primary. So he and his allies secured funding from large corporations like Chevron, Hilton, and Arco and got Proposition 21 on the ballot.

Unfortunately, after Wilson's campaign went down in flames, Proposition 21 lived on, even though its initial backers distanced themselves from it. They'd supported it only as long as it was a horse for their man Wilson to ride.

DJ: Why did it still pass?

CP: In part because voters have been primed with thirty years of anticrime propaganda. Crime has become the universal scapegoat and the best way to distract people from real problems.

But there's another factor that isn't discussed much on the Left, and that's the appeal of such laws at all levels of the class system. It's not just white suburban people voting for these tough-on-crime initiatives; it's working-class people and people of color in the inner city. So there's this incredible contradiction. These folks know the prisons don't work, the courts are racist, and the cops are violent, but if you ask what they want for their neighborhood, they say, "more cops." In part, this is because people in the inner city do face a real crisis of crime. Many of them are under siege by the criminal element in their own community. They want a solution.

But the solution they inevitably choose ties back into a folk authoritarianism that predates industrialism, coming down to us from the agrarian origins of our culture. It's characterized by a "common-sense" desire for and appreciation of discipline—including physical discipline—and has its roots in patriarchal notions of family and order. Those who step out of line are "bad children" who need to be taken behind the woodshed and "taught a lesson."

DJ: Getting back to the fiscal insanity of these programs: You mentioned that Proposition 21 will cost $5 billion and send thirty-eight thousand kids to adult prison. That's well over a hundred thousand dollars per kid.

CP: That's why the proposition was condemned by many of the players who normally come out for law and order—because it's insane overkill. Whenever polltakers told people how much Proposition 21 would cost, they opposed it.

With prisons, too, cost might become a real issue. People could start opposing incarceration because it's so expensive. Prison bonds are getting harder and harder to pass. But at the same time that voters are becoming less and less willing to fund incarceration, they claim to want more law and order. And the politicians can simply keep taxing the people and cutting social services to pay for prisons. For the time being, there seems to be plenty of money for incarceration, the same way there's always plenty of money for the military.

DJ: One of my students in the prison where I teach, a man in his early twenties, has been institutionalized since the age of eight. He just got out and doesn't know what he's going to do. He explicitly told me, "I don't care about anybody."

CP: An age-old critique of prisons is that they produce deviance. You send people into prisons—which some have called "universities of crime"—and they become damaged to the point where they need to be institutionalized forever. About half a million people are released from prison every year. Many of them hit the street economically and psychologically broken.

This is allowed to go on because it helps enforce class distinctions and racism. Fear of the crimes these men might commit sends people rushing into the arms of an increasingly authoritarian state. Citizens willingly surrender their rights and social power in exchange for protection.

Have you noticed, for instance, the degree to which surveillance is becoming an accepted feature of everyday life? As we move slowly toward a cashless economy, our movements and buying habits are being tracked by everyone from the government to Safeway—and we don't seem to mind. It's becoming increasingly natural. There's even direct surveillance. You drive across the Bay Bridge, and there's a camera taping you. You shop at a convenience store, and there's a camera. Many neighborhoods now have cameras recording activity on the streets.

I think we feel comfortable with this invasion of privacy because the threat is, for the moment, abstract: So what if Safeway wants to know what my demographic group does with its disposable income? So what if someone at the police station sees what time I walk my dog? But we seem to be forgetting that, if we allow the police and other elements of the prison-industrial-judicial complex too much power, we run the risk that these "bands of armed men" will slip the reins of democratic control. Most people, though, just don't see that as a possibility.

DJ: Who is supposed to police the police?

CP: Theory and practice are quite different on that question. We have all, of course, been taught about the checks and balances within our system. The judicial, legislative, and executive branches, for example, are set against one another. These checks and balances are supposed to let the state police itself. And the system works, to an extent. In the end, though, the people must police the state, and the way we do that is through social movements and varying degrees of rebellion.

It's important to remember that the government isn't all bad. The state is both an instrument of class control and an arena of class and social struggle. While social welfare institutions, for example, act as agents of control, they also redistribute wealth and help bring some modicum of fairness to capitalism. So the state is not a monolithic institution. It has different, sometimes competing, agendas.

In part, the current hardening of the American state—this shift toward authoritarianism—is due to the shift in the balance of power between its branches. The legislature, for example, is generally the most democratic part of the government, the place where the people can have the greatest influence, but recently we have seen the executive branch getting stronger and stronger. And we see the courts, which are so undemocratic in many ways, having more and more power over our daily life. And within the court system itself, power is shifting from judges and juries to prosecutors.

DJ: Yet in the struggle to save the environment, for example, the courts are just about the only branch of government that's helpful.

CP: That's why the Right constantly goes after the Endangered Species Act (ESA), which is enforced by the courts. It's not that the Right doesn't like birds and animals. Conservatives target the ESA because it threatens to become a loophole that could bring corporations to heel, or at least drive up their cost of operation.

In terms of criminal justice, however, the Prison Litigation Reform Act (PLRA), passed in 1996, has completely eviscerated the civil courts as an avenue of resistance for the people, particularly prisoners. Since then, it's become very hard to combat inhumane conditions in prison.

DJ: Why the evisceration?

CP: The right wing was beginning to run out of issues. I mean, what do you do once welfare is gone? Whom do you beat up on? Prisoners! Take their books, their weights, and, most of all, their access to the press and the courts. The PLRA's real function is to keep the female prisoners who've been raped by guards away from *Sixty Minutes*, to keep the tortured inmates out of court, and, best of all, to keep them all illiterate and without access to law books. Specifically, the PLRA forces prisoners to exhaust all administrative remedies before they can file suit and requires them to pay $120 every time they file a case. Most of them will never have that kind of money. In many states, the PLRA means no more law libraries, period. The list of restrictions goes on and on.

DJ: Let's talk about the SHUs—the Security Housing Units in California prisons. I don't think most people know about them.

CP: They have different names in different states. Basically, they're "supermax" lockdowns, prisons within prisons where inmates are kept in isolation—or sometimes with one cellmate—twenty-three hours a day. They live behind solid metal doors. Their only contact with the world is by way of a slot used to pass them their meals and through which their hands are cuffed before they go out on the exercise "yard"—a concrete floor and four concrete walls, with only a slice of sky above—or for their biweekly showers. Prisoners in these units are allowed only an hour or two of access to the law library each week and similarly limited access to telephones. They have no jobs, no educational programs, and can visit their families only through bulletproof glass, over bugged intercoms. They're watched twenty-four hours a day on closed-circuit TV, for years on end.

Like much of our current criminal justice system, supermax units are a product of the crisis of the sixties. They have earlier antecedents in Quaker prison reforms that advocated silence and isolation, and also in "the hole"—the dark room that prisoners are sent to in old prison movies. What's changed is that now people sometimes spend their entire sentences in the SHU, and the dark rooms have, in some cases, become sterile white boxes with canned air, electronic voices, and endless fluorescent light.

These modern isolation cells emerged in response to the prison yard rebellions and prisoners' rights movements of the sixties and seventies. At San Quentin, the first such units were called "adjustment centers" and were where the warden threw "incorrigible" nationalists, communists, and self-styled POWs. Nowadays, there are two ways you can get sent to the SHU. The first is if you're found guilty of violating the prison's rules, such as by possessing drugs or weapons. Then you can be given what's called a "determinate sentence," which means you're put in isolation for a term of months or years. The other way you can be sent to the SHU is if you're "validated" by the administration as a gang member. You then receive an "indeterminate sentence," which means you're in the SHU until either you die, your prison sentence ends, or you snitch on other gang members.

DJ: I've worked with prisoners who were in the SHU as long as eighteen years.

CP: That happens all the time.

DJ: And to be validated as a gang member is an administrative decision, totally nonjudicial.

CP: That's right. And it can be incredibly arbitrary. In the SHU, you'll find both serious gangsters and the political leaders of the prisoners. You'll also find jailhouse lawyers—self-taught legal advisors who write writs and sue on behalf of themselves and other prisoners. The SHU is full of brilliant legal minds who've been beating the California Department of Corrections—against all odds—with their lawsuits.

And now a new class is ending up in the supermax units: jailhouse doctors. A lot of prisoners who are HIV-positive have gotten indigent subscriptions to the *New England Journal of Medicine*, and some of them have become experts on HIV. These jailhouse doctors are helping other prisoners—some of whom can't read—to take care of themselves, telling them which combinations of drugs work and demanding new treatments from the prison medical staff, many of whom know less about HIV than these inmates. That causes trouble. In prison, the staff must be right, and the prisoners must be wrong. So you often find jailhouse doctors being labeled gang members and ending up in the SHU.

The public is sold the SHU and other lockdowns as tools to protect prisoners and guards from "super criminals," but the truth is that they actually destabilize the prison environment. If you take the knowledgeable, respected convicts away, you're left with a bunch of young hotheads struggling for control and influence. So the removal of convicts to the SHU actually leads to more violence.

Now, you might think it seems counterproductive for prison administrators to foster violence. But on a certain level, it makes perfect sense.

DJ: How so?

CP: Because infighting makes things easier for the guards. A former prisoner who's now a jail warden told me explicitly that if you've got two hundred people on a tier, it's a lot easier to control them if the tier is split into five mutually antagonistic factions. Prison administrators generally have a real interest in keeping prisoners at each other's throats, because then they're directing their violence toward one another, as opposed to directing it toward the staff or organizing to demand better treatment.

DJ: This reminds me of something I recently read in the paper: because of violence on the yard, wardens want more state money for devices that can detect weapons inside people's bodies. So, in a sense, prison unrest leads to greater funding.

CP: Exactly. There are so many ways that intra-inmate violence serves the interests of prison administrators.

The notion of devices to look inside people's bodies also makes me think of the way criminal justice surveillance insinuates itself into our lives; how fear is seeded throughout the culture until we all become institutionalized. French philosopher Michel Foucault came up with the notion of a "carcereal society," wherein we are subject to constant supervision by anonymous managers. His thesis is that, with the rise of capitalism, industrialization, and the modern nation-state, societal control has shifted away from spectacular assaults on the body, such as public executions, and toward interior methods—getting subjects to regulate themselves by internalizing authority. For Foucault, this shift is not evidence of improving human rights or moral progress, but rather of increasingly effective and pernicious mechanisms of social regulation.

And his thesis is true, to some extent, but what we've seen in the U.S., with the rise of our incipient police state, is in some ways a return to the spectacular uses of terror.

DJ: I'd say it's both.

CP: Yes, there's been a bifurcation according to socioeconomic class. The middle classes are controlled through the discourse of pathology, illness, and deviance. They more or less regulate themselves, reading the self-help magazines, policing their own psychology. They're under tremendous pressures to "function" better in society, to "realize their potential," to "maximize" health, to achieve "proper time management," and so on—anything to keep people on the straight and narrow and thus prevent the juggernaut from grinding to a halt.

The impoverished and dangerous classes, too, are subject to the discourse of psychology and social work, encouraged to "manage" themselves and "learn life skills." But that sort of talk can go only so far when it's not accompanied by social rewards. So in the post-welfare era, the poor are increasingly regulated through a modern version of old-fashioned terror. It's no longer public executions. Executions occur behind closed doors and are increasingly sanitized. The new source of terror is the policing of society, and of prisoners.

In *Lockdown America,* I describe SWAT teams' operations in Fresno as a kind of postmodern public execution—a highly ritualized, highly theatrical display of the sovereign's power. The SWAT teams operate in groups of thirty with helicopters for support. Like an invading army, they occupy whole neighborhoods, harass the residents, and surround the houses. They have machine guns, barking dogs, and armored personnel carriers. This is state propaganda, political theater, directed not at the "perp" holed up in the house, but at the hundreds of community members watching. There's a message being broadcast, a spectacular display of the power of the state. They'll wake you up in the middle of the night with a helicopter overhead, dogs barking, and someone yelling through a loudspeaker. You'll come out and see storm troopers carrying machine guns and wearing black fatigues and armor and helmets. It's about regulating people through the theatrics of terror.

DJ: Is the U.S. a police state?

CP: No, I would call the U.S. an *incipient* police state. A police state is one in which the military and the police control all the other state institutions, and repression has subordinated all other functions of the state. I don't think that's the case in the U.S.—yet. We do have an element of police state politics developing here, but I don't think we've arrived.

When you get caught up in the justice system and don't have any money, however, it might as well be a police state, because that's the way they treat you.

DJ: For me, as a white, middle-class male, it's not a police state at all, but for my students . . .

CP: They live in a totalitarian society.

DJ: My students call some prisoners POWs, because they're victims of the war on poor people and people of color.

CP: I wouldn't paint with such a broad brush, but I'm not living in the prison where you teach. There are political prisoners, and there are social prisoners, and then there are prisoners who become political on the inside, like jailhouse lawyers and jailhouse doctors, or the gang-truce organizers who end up in the SHU. They're definitely political prisoners of a sort.

DJ: Where does the Immigration and Naturalization Service (INS) fit into the incipient police state?

CP: The policing of immigrants is an important piece of the puzzle, and one that isn't talked about enough. Immigration is where the most pernicious forms of surveillance and interagency cooperation are occurring. The INS, local police, and the military are teaming up and using the latest technology to watch and control Mexicans and other Latinos. At first, this was done just at the border, but in the last four or five years, many of the projects developed in that political netherworld of border patrol have been imported wholesale into the U.S. For example, the INS is launching huge raids in the Midwest against an immigrant population with few legal rights and little access to the official language.

In 1990, the INS and the Border Patrol were authorized to enforce contraband and narcotics laws, which enabled them to conduct warrantless searches in border communities and even inland areas that were allegedly "vulnerable to air smuggling." Many conservative Americans would never have tolerated this had it not first been applied to illegal immigrants at the border.

The same laws and methods are increasingly being used against nonimmigrant populations. Take, for example, the High Intensity Drug Trafficking Areas, or HIDTAs, where there is military involvement, as well as a strange conglomeration of state, federal, and local law enforcement agencies empowered with special prosecutors. The first HIDTA was the border between Mexico and the U.S. Then an area encompassing all counties within 150 miles of that frontier was declared an HIDTA. Now there are seventeen HIDTAs, including New York and New Jersey, the San Francisco Bay Area, parts of the rural Northwest, and so on. These HIDTAs, with their questionable constitutionality and their indirect use of the military against the civilian population, no longer have anything to do with immigration; they're part of the paramilitary war on drugs.

DJ: But so what if the feds are watching drug runners?

CP: Let's be honest. This is not about interdiction. The U.S. cooperates time and again with major international drug runners like the Peruvian president Fujimori and the former president of Colombia. The top U.S. anti-drug officer in Colombia has just been indicted because he and his wife were importing heroin and laundering drug money. The CIA's been involved with drug running from the beginning. So there's no serious effort to keep drugs out of this country.

In any case, the war on drugs focuses on low- and mid-level players. And there are numerous ways in which even the mid-level players get off—for example, the assets forfeiture laws created in 1984. These laws allow the police to keep drug-tainted money and property they confiscate during drug operations. Far from encouraging police to go after upper-level drug dealers (who presumably would have more assets), these laws make it legal and easy for police to cut deals with the mid-level drug dealers they bust. They say, "We'll drop charges if you forfeit your seized property without going to court." The richer the drug dealers, the better the chance they'll just forfeit the cash they had lying around, and the police will drop the charges. The people who go to prison are, as always, the small-time dealers.

DJ: What other INS tactics are being brought to mainstream America?

CP: The use of biometrics—that is, computers that digitize fingerprints and search databases. Now it doesn't matter what name or Social Security number you give; if the authorities can get your fingerprint, they can instantly run it against all the fingerprints they've got on file. The vanguard of biometrics technology is in the INS, but it is increasingly being used by state and local law enforcement.

What we need to realize is that "the border"—in terms of state-sponsored repression—is no longer the geographic border. These technologies are not simply being used on "the other," but are becoming widespread. The whole idea of "the border" is blatantly racist. The interior enforcement by the INS is essentially an anti-Latino guest worker policing program. Imagine if it had been conceived and proposed in honest terms: "We'd like billions of dollars to set up a separate, parallel super-policing-and-detention system for people who are dark-skinned and do the jobs that nobody else wants."

DJ: Do you see any reason for hope?

CP: Quite a lot, actually. I'm heartened by the police accountability movement and the protests in New York City in response to the torture and sodomizing of Abner Louima and the murder of Amadou Diallo. Here in California, the movement against Proposition 21 was impressive. It created interesting coalitions and got a lot of young people involved. I hope that the scandal in the LAPD's anti-gang Rampart unit will galvanize people who might otherwise not care about the crimes of the police.

Perhaps these developments will help people begin to see the connections between different parts of the prison-industrial complex. This is about more than just bad cops and greedy interest groups, like guards' unions, wanting more money. The criminal justice system is an integral part of a larger political and economic system that depends on criminalizing the poor. Placing criminal justice and police power and prisons in the context of capitalist society as a whole allows us to see more openings through which to attack the problem, more places to engage the enemy, and more ways to resist.

KATHERINE ALBRECHT

Interview conducted
in fall 2003 and January 2004,
by telephone.

K atherine Albrecht is the director of CASPIAN (Consumers Against Supermarket Privacy Invasion and Numbering), an organization she founded in 1999 to advocate consumer-based solutions to the problem of retail privacy invasion. Katherine is widely credited with raising public awareness about Radio Frequency Identification (RFID) through CASPIAN's "Boycott Benetton" and "Boycott Gillette" campaigns, and through protest organizing, public appearances, and countless media interviews.

Albrecht is also widely recognized as one of the world's leading experts on consumer privacy. She has testified before the Federal Trade Commission, the California state legislature, the European Commission, and the Federal Reserve Bank, in addition to giving over a thousand television, radio and print interviews. Her efforts have been featured on CNN, NPR, the CBS *Evening News*, *Business Week*, the *London Times*, and many more. *Executive Technology Magazine* recently called Katherine "perhaps the nation's most outspoken privacy advocate," and *Wired* magazine has called her the "Erin Brockovich" of RFID.

Albrecht holds an undergraduate degree in international marketing and a master's degree in instructional technology. She is currently completing her doctorate in education at Harvard University, where she is writing her dissertation on consumer psychology and privacy issues.

Derrick Jensen: What is RFID?

Katherine Albrecht: RFID stands for Radio Frequency Identification ("RF" for Radio Frequency and "ID" for Identification, as in "ID card"). RFID is a new consumer goods tracking system that consists of tiny computer chips—the size in some cases of a speck of dust—hooked up to miniature antennas that can transmit information remotely. Industry wants to call them Smart Tags or "improved bar codes." We call them Spy Chips.

The international consortium that developed this technology wants to use these tiny chips to number and track every physical item on the entire planet. Obviously, this plan has profound implications for privacy.

DJ: How do these chips work?

KA: The typical RFID tag gets its power from energy sent to it through the air by reader devices in the environment. By itself, a passive RFID tag doesn't really do anything until it is contacted by a reader device that beams out electromagnetic energy (what you and I would call "radio waves"). The energy is picked up by the tag's antenna and transmitted to the chip, which then beams back its unique identifying number. It says, "Here I am. I am chip number 304862," and so on.

The numbering system they want to put on these chips is called the EPC, which stands for electronic product code. It's related to the UPC, or Universal Product Code, currently used as the bar code. The chip itself will contain ninety-six bits, which will provide enough unique combinations to number every product produced on the planet for at least a thousand years. Depending on which mathematician you ask, this is enough numbers to uniquely identify every grain of rice or every speck of sand on the planet.

The stated purpose is to enable every item to be identified and tracked at any point along a supply chain. The system could be applied to almost any physical item—from ballpoint pens to toothpaste to anything else. Each item would carry its own unique information coded into an embedded chip.

DJ: You're not talking about every can of Coke having the same identifying Universal Product Code, right?

KA: No, this is different. Today all cans of Coke have the same bar code number. But with RFID, every can of Coke would have its own unique, trackable code, different from every other can of Coke. So would every sweater, every pair of shoes, every tire, every dollar bill. Which means that anywhere there are reader devices, the item . . .

DJ: . . . and by extension anyone wearing or carrying it . . .

KA: . . . can be tracked. Right. And the plans for reader devices are pretty far-reaching. Proponents envision, in their words, a "pervasive global network" of millions of receivers along the entire supply chain—in airports, seaports, highways, distribution centers, warehouses, retail stores, and in the home. This would allow for seamless, continuous identification and tracking of physical items as they move from one place to another, enabling companies to determine the whereabouts of all their products at all times. An executive at International Paper put it bluntly, "We'll put a radio frequency ID tag on everything that moves in the North American supply chain." The ultimate goal is for RFID to create, as those behind it say, a "physically linked world" in which every item on the planet is numbered, identified, catalogued, and tracked.

The technology already exists to make this a reality. Creating this global system is described by its backers as "a political rather than a technological problem." Supporters are aiming for worldwide acceptance of the technologies needed to build the infrastructure within the next few years.

This technology is slated to replace the bar code, so we should talk a little more about that. There are three fundamental ways RFID is different from a bar code. As I said, unlike a bar code, where the UPC numbers on your can of Coke would match the numbers on my can of Coke, each can of Coke rolling off the assembly line will be issued its own unique identifying number. The concern here is that when you pay for that can of Coke, its unique ID number will be linked up with your name in the store's database. This is already happening today. Any time you pay with a credit card, ATM card or check, the store records who you are and every item you bought, and that information gets consolidated into giant multi-store databases. Now imagine that instead of recording that you bought Coke, like they do today, the store records which exact, specific cans of Coke you bought. Store databases will become giant registration systems that can cross reference the owner of any physical item purchased on the planet. Everything you own could be linked specifically to you in a database.

If you take that to the next step it means that any item in the world can be picked up and scanned and its owner identified. So if a can of Coke falls off the garbage truck on the way to the dump and someone picks it up, they could scan it and you could get an automatic littering ticket in the mail. Or someone could steal the can of Coke and plant it at a crime scene and you could get a knock on your door asking what you were doing last night. It means that when you give someone a gift, the ownership trail could be tracked. If you're wearing a watch given to you by your ex-girlfriend, as you walk through a doorway you could be identified through things you bought and her connection with you could also be inferred based on your carrying something registered to her.

DJ: So if I had any purchased consumer item on me, if I wore clothes that were manufactured, I could be tracked at every moment?

KA: Right. You could be tracked by the things you carry. Once we move away from anonymous cash, which will happen very soon if we are not careful, it will be impossible to make a purchase without being identified. And the reason they want you to be identified is because they want to track the things you buy, and ultimately they want to track you.

The second way RFID tags are different from bar codes is that they can be read from a distance, right through the things we normally rely on to protect our privacy, like a backpack, or a shopping bag, or a suitcase. Radio waves travel through virtually any material but metal or water. This sets on its head a basic, fundamental, common sense, human body notion of what creates privacy—that if you can't see it, you don't know about it. If I have something private—a book I don't want you to know I'm reading, a package of condoms, a spare pair of underwear, or anything else I don't want to advertise to the world—I can put it in my purse or my pocket. And people won't know what's in there. RFID changes that, because in essence it creates a form of X-ray vision so that anyone with access to the technology can know what I'm trying to hide. That's so counterintuitive that people sometimes have a difficult time understanding it could be done to them.

It also entirely throws out the notion of consent. These things can be read at a distance, through fabric, without your knowledge or permission. It's possible that every doorway you walk through could be equipped with a reader device that would take a full inventory of everything you're wearing and carrying. And you would never know it was happening. It is possible that every park bench you sat on—they've actually talked about embedding these in furniture—would be able to identify you and what is in your lunch bag.

At this point people always ask, who would want to do this and why? The researchers at MIT who developed this technology were working for a consortium of multinational corporations and government agencies that funded them. It took them three years and millions of dollars. And of course now that RFID exists, uses quickly start springing into people's minds. Look at who is interested in these technologies. Does the Defense Department have your best interests at heart? How about Wal-Mart?

There's a third way RFID is unlike bar codes. To the best of my knowledge there's no serious health impact from exposure to bar code readers and laser scanners unless you stare at the laser. But there may be quite worrisome health problems associated with being continually bombarded by RFID electromagnetic energy from the reader devices. Even today if you go into certain Target stores to buy DVDs with RFID tags attached you could be standing next to a shelf that's bombarding you with electromagnetic energy.

The proponents of this technology say there are no health risks, that it's no more dangerous than being near an FM radio. Well, they're being disingenuous there, too, because their internal documents reveal that they contacted scientists and government committees from countries all over the world to ask for their latest research, opinions, and laws on electromagnetic energy. What emerges is a widely diverging set of opinions over whether or not this technology is safe. The basic conclusion of the Auto-ID center scientists was, "We don't know, and maybe we should do a little more research." That's great. I think they *should* do a little more research. But that's not the standard industry line, and in the meantime they're proceeding full-steam ahead. Even with their self-confessed need for more research, they want to put these things literally *everywhere*. What effects will this have on pregnant women and growing children and the elderly? What about the rest of us? Do we want to be constantly probed by electromagnetic waves looking for anything that could provide them with information about us? It's not only creepy, it's quite possibly dangerous.

DJ: Who is behind this?

KA: In 1999, a group called the Auto-ID Center (and that's "auto" for automatic, not automotive) was formed at the Massachusetts Institute of Technology to make RFID small enough, efficient enough and cheap enough to tag everything. It was a partnership between Gillette, Procter & Gamble, and MIT, and later counted one hundred of the world's biggest corporations and government departments as "members." These include product-manufacturing companies like Philip Morris, Coca-Cola, Kimberly Clark, Johnson and Johnson, and Kraft; and retailers like Wal-Mart, Target, Home Depot, and the British chain Tesco. International Paper, which packages a huge percentage of the goods sold in this country, is a sponsor, and so is UPS. Within the government you've got the Department of Defense and the U.S. Postal Service, and more recently, Homeland Security. Very big players are behind this technology.

In 2001 this gang wired the city of Tulsa, Oklahoma, to see if they could track objects tagged with RFID. Gillette, Wal-Mart, and Tesco have installed shelves that can read RFID tags embedded in razor packages. The shelves take shoppers' photographs when they pick the items up off the shelf. The European Central Bank and the government of Japan are both working on plans to imbed bank notes—cash—with RFID tags to make it as traceable as credit cards, and no longer anonymous. Hitachi Europe has already developed a chip small enough, at 0.3 mm square and thin as a human hair, to fit inside a banknote. Mass production of these chips has already begun.

DJ: How did this RFID get started?

KA: Proponents like to claim that RFID technology has been around since World War II, when it was used to distinguish enemy warplanes from friendly planes. "It's an old technology, nothing to see here, move along folks," they say. It's funny how technologists will try to make even the most outrageous thing seem commonplace—or permanently entrenched—by saying "oh, that? It's been around forever." And a lot of us buy into it.

It's an important phenomenon. I remember a few years back seeing a photograph of a perfectly formed human ear growing out of the back of a living mouse. I was so horrified that the room spun. I immediately called a friend of mine saying we had to *do* something about it. How could we allow scientists to create such monstrosities? When I reached him, my friend said, "I can't believe you are just now seeing that photo. It's been around for ages. Where have you been?" Amazingly, that response shut me right up; all my fury fizzled on the spot. Instead of feeling angry, I felt stupid—stupid, then crushingly defeated. Why? How does our society get us to replace acute, healthy outrage with a chronic, there's-nothing-we-can-do-about-it, soul-killing ache?

My experience watching the RFID industry has clued me in to part of the answer. The technologists' dirty trick is to convince us that we can only fight things that are new. If something has been around for a while, the implication is that other people have already accepted it (or so they want you to think). At that point, anyone opposing a particular development can be dismissed for being "behind the times" (though that's rarely the case), or for arguing about something that's already been settled in the court of public opinion (though it rarely has been).

This is dangerous because it means that industry can quietly slip something into the world and not mention it for a year or so, outside of a few esoteric industry publications. When regular people eventually find out about it, their outrage is siphoned away as industry reps stifle a yawn and say, "Oh, please, that old technology? It has been around for ages. Where have you been?" Then suddenly you're the one on the defensive.

This has not been the case with opposition to RFID. We found out about it in the earliest planning stages a few years back, when I attended meetings at the Auto-ID Center and heard firsthand, behind closed doors, what they were developing. It must have been frustrating to the RFID folks that the standard "oh, please, let's not rehash that old thing" line wouldn't work in this situation, which is why I think they later tried to paint it as having been around for sixty years.

When that didn't work, they reversed tactics and started saying that opposition to RFID is premature since the technology is too new to judge. It's hilarious. When you respond early you're "jumping the gun," but if you wait even a fraction of a second after that, you're "beating a dead horse." They've rigged the game so there is *never* a good time to criticize technology.

And in the case of RFID, it's nuts to say it dates back to World War II in any meaningful sense. The first commercial application of the kind of small, efficient, passive EPC tags we're talking about now came in November, 2002, when Gillette announced it was going to buy 500 million of them from a company called—and I'm not making this up—Alien Technology.

DJ: I'm a little confused about the technology. What's the difference between a chip and a tag?

KA: That's a good question, since a lot of people get them confused. An RFID tag is a combo unit consisting of an RFID chip and the antenna it's connected to. When you're talking about RFID, you're nearly always talking about a tag, since neither a chip nor an antenna alone can do much. The chip is the tiny piece of silicon, the little wafer, the computer chip that can be as small as a speck of dust. Currently the smallest one is Hitachi's mu chip at only 0.3 millimeters square. Hitachi's website has a picture of a magnified grain of rice with a tiny black speck on it—the mu chip. So they can get quite small.

The chip contains data, but in order to communicate the data at a distance it has to be hooked up to an antenna. The antenna is typically made of a flat strip of metal (although they're experimenting with various other materials). It's designed to pick up and amplify any ambient electromagnetic energy beamed at it by an RFID reader. The readers emit a continual stream of energy on the chance that an RFID tag might be within range. If the reader pings an RFID tag, the tag's antenna picks up the energy and stimulates the chip to beam its data back to the reader device. That's how it all works. And that's where their "pervasive global network of reader devices" comes in. A reader device can be placed almost anywhere. They can be installed in doorways, woven into carpet, and hidden under floor tiles. They can be embedded in the asphalt of roads.

They've even talked about putting them into the refrigerators and medicine cabinets in our homes.

While RFID chips are very small, they get connected to antennas to make tags that are a lot bigger. The smallest tags I've seen with any kind of range are maybe the size of my thumbnail. Most are larger. But researchers are working on ways to turn a product's packaging itself into the antenna. I've been told that International Paper, for example, can put an RFID tag between layers of cardboard so a consumer would have no knowledge it's there. A company called Flint Ink has developed a spray-on metallic-based RFID antenna that just looks like ink. They can put the tiny chip on top of a gray matte-looking surface, then cover it with regular packaging ink and you'd never even see it.

Also, you know how a lot of packages today, particularly Procter & Gamble products, incorporate a shiny foil surface on top of the cardboard? They're working to make that function as a fully active RFID antenna, too. This means that the RFID chip could anywhere on the package and as hard to find as a tiny speck of dust. It could actually be the dot of the "i" on the fine print on the back and you'd never know it. Fortunately, today most RFID tags are big enough to be seen, but that is going to change fairly shortly.

We should also talk about the read range of these tags—how close you have to be to read one. Most of the cheaper tags that will be mass-produced to replace the bar code rely on energy from the reader like I just described. They're called "passive" tags because they passively wait for a reader to tell them what to do. Their read range is limited to somewhere between a couple of inches and twenty or thirty feet. But you can attach a battery to an RFID tag and make what's called an "active" tag. This can increase the read range to extraordinary distances. In fact, with a powerful enough battery, you can beam the information over miles.

The batteries can be any size, really, though a more powerful battery usually means a longer read range. The challenge is to get the batteries small enough and cheap enough so they can be widely used. The latest breakthrough is a flat, printed battery less than a millimeter thick that can be used to power active RFID tags. It looks a lot like an adhesive sticker, and you can buy them in rolls. The company that makes these batteries suggests building them into credit cards and putting them "discreetly" on cereal boxes. Can you imagine your cornflake box beaming information about you down the block?

DJ: Why are they doing this?

KA: Well, as the co-director for the Auto-ID center said to an interviewer for the BBC (and I'm paraphrasing), "In the past, the chain of getting stuff to the store was like a person whose arm ended at the elbow, in that we just didn't have that reach into really knowing everything. But an RFID-enabled store will be like a nervous system that extends all the way down to the tips of the fingers." I thought that was such a vivid and appropriate image. These tentacles, these fingers, are reaching into every aspect of knowing where things are.

DJ: Once again, why are they doing this?

KA: There are really two different camps as to what they'd like to do with RFID. One wants to use it to enhance security by putting RFID tags in our identity documents, in building passes, even in our flesh to make it easy to track people's comings and goings and to make sure that only "authorized" people get access to certain areas and information. Others want to use it in the supply chain—in warehouses, distribution centers and manufacturing plants—so they can keep track of inventory while it's in their possession. Of course, with physical items the question becomes, what happens when we buy those things? Will they still be trackable? That's where the two camps, tracking you and tracking everything you own, merge. In other words, the goal is total surveillance.

Right now I'm sitting on my back porch. I see a wading pool, a hammock, a basket that used to hold flowers. I see plastic deck chairs. When I bought all these things they had bar codes with UPCs. None of them have bar codes anymore because I pulled the stickers off and threw them away. In the new world where you have RFID chips instead of bar codes, the RFID would not be stuck on as plastic stickers, but instead would be extruded into the plastic or woven into the item in the manufacturing process. Every one of the things on my porch would probably still contain an RFID chip and be readable from across my yard.

And the chips are virtually indestructible. They can sit in the sun, they can go through the washer and the dryer. They're already being used in people's uniforms, and can last for years of high temperature industrial washing and drying with no problem. They're difficult to get rid of and can be nearly impossible to detect. Do you want these in your clothing?

But there is something even greater at stake here. The image I have surrounding RFID is of a palpable, tangible, power-hungry negative force. And I'm not just talking about RFID. I'm talking about this whole culture, this whole impulse that is destroying our planet and harming humans and nonhumans everywhere. RFID is the inevitable next point in that kind of all-seeing, all-knowing, all-controlling, all-destroying kind of a culture. It's indicative of an intent, a mindset. RFID is intrinsic to that.

I recently had a discussion about this with my husband. He said, "You know, Katherine, the technology in itself is not evil. It's only evil when you combine it with this culture."

I said, "What do you mean? This technology is clearly terrible."

He responded, "Well, how would this technology be applied in a freedom-loving, limited-government, libertarian kind of state? How could you use it?"

DJ: I would say that such a government could never exist, since the primary purpose of government is to provide the muscle to enable the rich to steal resources from the poor and from the land; to protect the rich from the outrage of the poor; and further, to rationalize exactly the sort of control we are talking about. That said, I think I see his point.

KA: I said, "Well, maybe you put RFID tags on all the cops so you'd know when they were coming near you. Or all the government agents would be forced to wear these devices so you could tell when they might be about to oppress or spy on you." The point is that you'd use it in the opposite way. You'd use it to protect and preserve freedom. You'd use it to minimize the power of those who would wield too much power.

DJ: The reason this can't happen is that our entire culture is based on this imbalance of power. That's the strength of Jeremy Bentham's Panopticon. It is a prison design where the cells radiate from a central tower, such that there are no nooks and crannies where the guards cannot see. The cells are always kept lit and the guard tower is always kept dark. Thus the surveillance is always possible, never verifiable. And it goes only one way. Of course the Panopticon isn't just a design for a prison, but for a whole carcereal society.

KA: There are those—and I think they're wrong—who think the answer to so much surveillance is more surveillance. David Brin, for example. He's got a book out that a lot of people seem to be agreeing with that says if they're going to watch us we need to watch them. His solution seems to be that if you somehow make all the rich people's lives transparent, and the government transparent, so everything everybody does is known to everybody else, there will be no more opportunity for abuse.

DJ: That's just plain silly. Not only does he ignore everything we know about power dynamics, but . . .

KA: . . . But even if it were remotely possible it creates a world I don't think most of us would want to live in.

DJ: Why not? What's the big deal with having chips everywhere? If you have nothing to hide, who cares? If all you do is buy stuff from Safeway and Albertson's anyway—so long as you're not a fricking drug dealer—why do you care if there are chips in money?

KA: I used to bristle whenever I heard that. But then I realized the proper response: if I have nothing to hide, why the heck are you spying on me? If I have done nothing wrong, leave me alone.

DJ: But they're not targeting you! It's not personal. It's just going to be in your underwear.

KA: I can answer that from a couple of perspectives. First, let me answer it using my doctoral research in psychology. Studies have shown a couple of interesting things about privacy and human psychology. One is that about 25 percent of people oppose privacy invasion and will fight to protect their autonomy. Another 25 percent are at the opposite end of the spectrum, welcoming the idea of being surveilled and losing their autonomy. They're the ones who say, "Put a camera in my shower, put a camera in my toilet, bring it on, I can take it." And then there are 50 percent in the middle who are very practical, and who say, "Show me what's in it for me. Where's the benefit? Where's the harm?" Those percentages haven't changed, even with the development of new technology. The other finding is even more interesting. Study after study has shown that when you take away people's privacy—when you give them the impression that they could be watched at any time—even if they're doing nothing "wrong," and even if the watching is supposedly benign, the people end up being really neurotic. They end up becoming paranoid.

One reason the Panopticon is so effective is that if you don't know when and where you're being watched, your mind plays tricks on you and you start inventing surveillance scenarios. Human beings are, like it or not, highly social creatures. We are finely attuned to the way other people perceive us. And if we never have an opportunity to just be, to let our hair down, undo the top button or whatever it is we do to relax when we know we're not being watched, we start to go nuts. People have to have that sense of being able to relax without putting on the social face. So constant surveillance is not only a problem for obvious political and philosophical reasons, but it's also a very real problem for psychological and psychiatric reasons: it's quite unhealthy to be constantly surveilled.

We're starting to see a lot of that. I get a lot of phone calls from people who are convinced they've been implanted with listening devices by the government, or the government is speaking into their head . . .

DJ: . . . in ways even more direct than television . . .

KA: Ha, exactly. Or they say that aliens have planted things inside of them. Given the surveillance that now characterizes our way of living, and given the known effects of such constant surveillance on people's psyches, I think we can easily expect to see more and more of that.

DJ: You used the word "paranoid" a minute ago, but frankly, given the way the technology is moving . . .

KA: There is nothing now that is outside the realm of possibility, in terms of abuse. And that's exactly the problem.

DJ: Having said all that, I can also hear in my head the counterarguments: do you want your kid to be kidnapped and never be seen again? Well, put a little chip in your child's neck. And I've heard so many people say to me, "Well, chips in people are a terrible idea, but you know, my kids just got their driver's licenses, so maybe they could be good." Let's go back to the basic argument always thrown out by proponents of universal surveillance: "If you're not doing anything wrong, you've got nothing to worry about." What's wrong with that?

KA: The question that must *always* be asked about this is, who decides what is right or wrong? Who gave the people behind these schemes the right to make these choices for the rest of us? So often when we believe we've been given a choice, we've been lied to. When people say, "If you're not doing anything wrong, you have nothing to fear" they're really saying, "If you're not going against the wishes of those in power, you have nothing to fear." Which is an entirely different thing.

There are times when it is appropriate not to do what you are told, because to do what you are told is to do terrible things. Think of hiding Anne Frank in your attic. "Well, if you're doing nothing wrong, then you have nothing to hide, and nothing to fear." Well, was it wrong to hide her and her family? To not hide them properly, which in some ways is what happened, was to cause her and her whole family to be murdered by state psychopaths. Or what about the Underground Railroad? If Harriet Tubman weren't doing anything wrong, she would have had nothing to hide. But Harriet Tubman broke the law by rescuing slaves and helping them escape. She carried opiates with her, and she carried a gun. The opiates were to calm the people she was transporting in case they got too frightened, and the gun was to shoot them if they wouldn't stop screaming. Here was someone operating in gross violation of what we would consider to be the law, and yet she did some extraordinary things through a terrible time. And now in retrospect she's written up in fourth grade textbooks as a heroine.

If the power is wrong, sometimes fighting the power is the right thing to do.

Here's something. A marijuana legalization group recently placed ads on public buses, then some lawmaker tried to stop them by making it a crime to place ads promoting illegal activity. Remember, there was a time when it was illegal for women to vote, so women campaigning for the right to vote would have been in violation of that law. Putting up a poster saying, "We women would like the right to vote, respectfully, please," would have been a crime.

We've come to the point in this culture where even asking for change, or for the removal of draconian restrictions—think of attempting to end segregation—becomes a crime in and of itself. A simple effort to educate others, to see if the status quo couldn't be changed, becomes a crime.

Who gives them permission to treat us this way?

In the last couple of days I've been thinking a lot about the permission issue. I'm working with a reporter on a story about how corporations and governments gather certain types of information in a way they shouldn't, in such a way that people have no idea they're giving information for purpose A and it's being used for purpose B. There are hundreds of examples of that. Now, for example, merchants can use your cell phone to identify you as you walk into a store. This was written up in *Wired* in December. Stores can have little reader devices that pick up information on your cell phone. The stores can then link that information with your cell phone records, the records that you gave the cell phone company for the service, and use that to identify you, and to identify your potential tastes and other information about you, and use that to market products to you.

Did you know that these days in order to get a cell phone you have to give your social security number? Why do they need that? My husband was willing to pre-pay a couple of hundred dollars so the company wouldn't have to worry about him racking up calls to Zimbabwe, but the cell phone company still demanded a social security number or they wouldn't give him a phone. He refused to give it, and some people might have said he was crazy, paranoid: "What's your cell phone company going to do with your social security number?" But as so often happens, the thing that at first seems paranoid ends up being right on.

That's true not just with cell phones but with so many things. If you want to live your life where you are not constantly being surveilled—and frankly where you're not getting screwed at every turn—you have to live your life almost as an outcast from society.

Just yesterday I had an argument about these issues with a medical practitioner. Apparently for standard practice of care I was supposed to have blood test X. I was thinking, "I probably know a lot more than you do about the potential privacy downsides of having blood test X." I said, "Did you know that there are entire genetic repositories of people's blood being collected from blood tests like this?" She looked at me like I'd gone mad, and said, "I can't continue to be your medical practitioner unless you consent to these tests." And I said, "We may have to talk about that then, because I'm not going to do it."

Who gave them permission to collect this data? If I'm getting a blood test for a legitimate reason, what right do they have to put my blood into some genetic databank for who-knows-what eventual reason?

DJ: This makes me think of the line from the document "Rebuilding America's Defenses," put out by the Project for a New American Century, an organization that includes Vice President Dick Cheney, Secretary of Defense Donald Rumsfeld, the president's brother Jeb Bush, and Paul Wolfowitz, generally considered the mastermind behind the invasion of Iraq, where the authors state that "advanced forms of biological warfare that can 'target' specific genotypes may transform biological warfare from the realm of terror to a politically useful tool."

KA: So wouldn't it be helpful for them to know not only the genetic makeup of people living on land that has resources on or beneath it, but also to have the phenotype and blood information for people who refuse to fall in line, for those damn squeaky wheels, those nails that refuse to be pounded in? What makes them different from everyone else? What about that 25 percent of people who do not want to be surveilled? Is it something in their physical makeup? And if so, can we—those in power—do something to "fix" that?

At some point it might be possible to identify compliant versus non-compliant people in the womb. Imagine if someday this became part of a standard prenatal blood panel performed on the mom. There will be questions: "Who is going to be an acceptable member of society? Who may create a few too many problems for the power structure?" Of course they won't be phrased that way. Instead it will be, "Who will be antisocial? Who will be a threat to society, to their parents, and to themselves?"

So, who gave them permission? I didn't. Did you?

Oh, here's something I was reading just today. It also was also in *Wired*. They quoted Paco Underhill, the guy who founded a company called EnviroSell, which has used recording equipment to spy on people in Denny's while they read the menu and hires fake shoppers to pretend to shop in stores while they're really just recording information about other shoppers. (They look just like normal people but they're not; they're the Borg!) His website has an FAQ with questions like, "Isn't it illegal to tape record and videotape people without their permission?" The response is, "Oh, no, most people think that, but it's perfectly legal." Evidently it's a misperception that most of us have that it's illegal to surreptitiously and secretly video and audiotape people in public spaces such as sit-down restaurants (like Denny's). Underhill states—and I have to say he does this almost gleefully—that when you're in public, you have an expectation of being seen and heard. And thus recorded. Another question on the website: "Won't people notice the cameras?" His response: "Most people are so intent on the shopping experience that they don't notice the cameras, and if they do, they just think they're part of a shoplifting prevention program." He also says, "Occasionally kids will notice it." Children are the ones who tend to be aware of it, and point it out.

And isn't that the way it so often is, that children are the ones who point out what is pathological about your society? Children will look at you and say, "Mom, I don't get why it is that I'm supposed to be kind to animals and yet it's okay to do experiments on them. I'm confused. Explain that to me, Mom."

And usually the adults respond, "Oh, don't go there, Junior." They get the brush off. They get the non-explanation. They get the uncomfortable red-faced parent shifting from foot to foot. Because they haven't absorbed the craziness yet, it's children who are often able to get right to the heart of what is fundamentally wrong with society.

DJ: Which is undoubtedly one reason for all the surveillance in schools these days. It's really clear to me that a primary purpose of that is simply to get kids used to the ubiquity of surveillance, so they won't ask those questions. It has nothing to do with whether someone is going to sneak into the cafeteria to steal mystery meat.

KA: It serves a really powerful purpose in that. On that topic, there's a store in a lot of American shopping malls, a big publicly-traded company making tons of money, called "Build-A-Bear." These stores have machines that build Teddy Bears while kids watch. The machines toss stuffing in the air, put it in, sew on the arms, and so on. The kids are supposed to form a lifetime relationship bond with these bears. Because the point is to make money off these kids, the stores of course sell accessories.

A friend went to one of these stores recently, and pointed out that the store he went to was right next to a pet store selling live puppies. He said, "What's the difference? The live puppy comes with its live puppy accessories, and the Build-A-Bear comes with its weird bear accessories." It's all tied in.

I bring up Build-A-Bear because we were talking about how the culture conditions children to accept constant surveillance. When your child is at the final phase of creating her Build-A-Bear, the store clerk drops a bar coded ID tag into it. Inside. Embedded in there. And the clerk says to her, "This is because you really love your bear, and you never want to lose your bear, and if you ever lost your bear, and someone else found it, we could scan this little tag, and bring your bear home to you! We're going to fill out this (very detailed) registration, which will have who you are, and your birth date and where you live. It's like a birth certificate for your bear! Isn't that wonderful!" Of course under these circumstances I can't imagine many kids saying no to a tracking device—an ID implant—in their bear.

I think about these little girls somewhere down the road, when they're in the hospital giving birth, and I imagine someone saying to them, "Well, you loved your little Build-A-Bear, and if you love little Junior here, you're going to want to keep track of him, too. What if he gets kidnapped? If you love your kid, you've got to put an RFID implant into him."

DJ: I'm sure you're aware that there are already people voluntarily implanting themselves with chips so they don't have to carry credit cards.

KA: Yes, unfortunately, the implant is already here. So the message is that if you love your child, you will implant her with a tracking device. But what if you oppose tracking devices because they're dehumanizing? Or your religion forbids it? Or for any reason? The implication is that not only do you not love your child, but you are a killer. Here's the headline from this month's issue of *ID-Tech EX*: "Privacy Groups with Blood on their Hands." And here's a quote, "Never forget that privacy advocates have some very nasty bedfellows. Those that wish to make false warranty claims, fraudulent product returns, thieves, pursue piracy and smuggling, kill people with counterfeit pharmaceuticals, and steal babies from hospitals, for instance. The U.S. has twenty-five thousand mother/baby mismatches in hospitals every year. Should we help the baby stealers and do nothing about the errors by staff that cause this? The bottom line to remember: that you know people by the company they keep. And as they seek their moment of fame, privacy advocates assist some very questionable people. Of course they have some valid arguments in a minority of cases, but there are few, if any, concrete examples of privacy abuse with RFID that should have been avoided."

So, now I'm a co-conspirator with baby thieves? This is absolutely insane. But the idea that people who care about privacy want to see people's babies be kidnapped is what they're going to tell those little girls who right now at age seven and eight are watching little ID tags get implanted in their teddy bears.

Let's take this baby thief accusation head on. The problem, they say, is that there are twenty-five thousand mother/baby mismatches every year. But why would you have twenty-five thousand mother/baby mismatches? Because they're all in these industrial production units called hospitals, cranking out babies that are immediately separated from their mothers and put into holding tanks with tons of other babies. Can you imagine any other culture doing this? How could you possibly mix up a baby? How could babies be going to a place where they could be mixed up? How could we as a culture have gotten to such a point? You have your baby, you hold your baby, you love your baby, you sleep with your baby, you cuddle your baby, your baby is never out of your sight. Why would my baby get lost or mixed up with somebody else's baby?

Within a system and a mindset that leads to twenty-five thousand mother/baby mismatches, it may make sense to implant your baby with a tracking device. Outside this system, it's all horrifyingly insane.

Why is it that these people come up with really hideous solutions that put the burden on us to solve the problems they created in the first place?

DJ: The question I keep asking is: Who's in charge? Technology critics for many years have pointed out that technology drives this discussion—not the desires of the people, not ecological sanity, but technology and the urge to control.

KA: That's a pattern that goes way back in this culture.

I know that part of the problem right now is that there is effectively no consumer movement in this country, and therefore no one is pushing for controls. There's a lot of hand wringing on the part of journalists, but—and somebody may take me to task for saying this because they may view themselves as part of a consumer movement—the consumer movement in this country is flat dead. Part of what I'm trying to do is revive that.

It's astonishing how different things are now than in the 1970s. Back then, thanks in great measure to Ralph Nader and to a political climate of citizen empowerment, there was a huge consumer movement in this country. Just the other day I was reading a book from around 1976, about whether your older children should be at the birth of your new child. It's a very 1970s kind of book, with the very 1970s kind of commune feel to it. It's lovely, but very outdated.

DJ: It's very groovy.

KA: Exactly. It's got this feel of, if we all just hold hands and love each other then everything will be okay. But the point is that there's a chapter in there on consumerism. What does consumerism have to do with whether your children should be at your birth? Well, it's the sort of obligatory chapter that everything in the 1970s had, this idea that you're a consumer, that it's your money paying for your health care, paying for the birth of your baby. You should be empowered. And *that* is the point: It's all about empowerment. It's all about standing up to demand your rights. You shouldn't be pushed around by health care providers, because you are the consumer, and you're the king.

With that mindset prevalent, it would have been difficult for RFID tracking and other abusive things to happen, not because of regulation and laws, but because people had a sense of empowerment and entitlement, and a sense of, "What do you mean, you're going to do X? You don't have a right to do X because I'm the consumer and I'm the king."

In the 1970s every major university had a department of consumer education. Elementary and junior high schools across the country had courses in consumerism. There were so many consumer textbooks that programs were designed simply to evaluate them all.

Those of us in our generation, who only caught the tail end of it, don't generally realize how powerful that movement was. Yet the vast majority of the standards that are now in place to protect consumers were put into place at that time. Unfortunately for us now, at that time none of this technology existed. So here we are limping along with an understanding of the consumer world that dates back to 1978. Since then nothing has been done to address the huge coercion and power imbalances and outright abuse that has been happening. Nobody is doing it. There are people, bless their hearts, who are trying. But there is no major movement. And that's what we need.

DJ: Where do you see this all headed?

KA: My answer usually depends on whether you ask me on a good or bad day. I have received two hundred thousand emails from people around the world (most of them come from the U.S.), and these letters reveal a huge sense of discontent. It feels like when the leaves start to rustle and the air feels a certain way right before you have a big storm. This rustling crosses political, religious, and ideological chasms you'd think would never be crossed. And they're all saying the same thing: something *has* to be done, or we are really doomed. I get this from lawyers, professors, farmers, students, everybody.

We're all sensing we're on the brink of something, but what?

People are really unhappy with the way things are going. Sure, there's a sizable chunk of people who are oblivious and who will always be oblivious and would have been oblivious through any period of history and through any social change. But they're not the people who are going to make anything happen. The people who are going to make things happen are feeling a need to do that now.

So where is it going?

Well, if we don't change something, there will be a camera in every bathroom, an RFID tag in every person's hand. It's going to go to total surveillance. That's the trajectory we're on. Where your every word can be listened to, whether you're in your car, at work, on the phone, or having an intimate moment with your spouse. All of that will be an open book to people who want to know it.

And who will want to know it?

Those with an authoritarian temperament, those who believe that if it comes from an authority, it's right. C. S. Lewis has this great story in one of his books, about a man working in the government schools who comes to him and complains, "The higher ups are just ridiculous, and they put these irrelevant bureaucratic mandates on us that interfere with our work. It's terrible. They're all a bunch of power-hungry creeps. None of this has anything to do with us doing our jobs." A couple of months later, C. S. Lewis sees this guy again and asks how things are going. The guy says, "Oh, I've been promoted. Everything is great now."

There's a whole portion of our society that may groan and gripe about the power structure if they're not at the top of it, but their solution is to claw their way to the top. Not to fix it. I think that's what we're up against. Those are the people who do great with public school indoctrination and other forms of getting people to think in approved ways.

DJ: There are so many ways the culture gets us to stay in line. A couple of years ago I was in an airport, and a security person put her hand inside my pants. I asked her what she was doing. She responded, "This is for your safety and the safety of others." I said, "You putting your hand inside my pants doesn't make anyone safer." She said, "Flying is a privilege, not a right. If you don't like it, stay home." I began to disagree, and she motioned to a nearby cop. I had a plane to catch, and so I had a choice: I could make a scene, or I could get the hell out of Austin, Texas. I got the hell out of Austin, Texas.

KA: That's how it goes. Food stamp applicants are forced to give information they may not want to give—information not relevant to the process—and if they balk, they're told, "Food stamps are a voluntary program. If you don't want to give the information, don't apply." Why are you crying about giving your social security number for a cell phone? Just don't get a cell phone. Nobody's putting a gun to your head and forcing you to connect. But have you noticed how hard it's getting to find a pay phone lately?

DJ: So don't make telephone calls. Making telephone calls is a privilege, not a right.

KA: Okay, so I won't make any more phone calls, I won't get any medical care, I won't go to the grocery store, I won't travel.

That's how the system works. Everywhere you go you've got to comply or forfeit your ability to do X. And sometimes your ability to do X is really critical, like your ability to buy food. That's what we're going to come down to.

The whole food thing is interesting. I want to tell you about a prediction I made a few years back concerning those grocery club cards. I said that at some point there would be a scare in the food supply, and that those in power will use it to mandate a system to record all food purchases in this country. Here's how I said it would play out. There will be some disease or toxic threat to the food supply. At that point, shopper cards will be presented as the savior.

DJ: How?

KA: People who have "registered" their purchase of recalled toxic item X by scanning a shopper card will be notified and be able to get the stuff out of their cupboard or fridge in time to save themselves and their children. There will probably be a few high profile cases of people who die, either because they didn't use a card so their purchase wasn't in the database, or—play your violin here—because they shopped at a store that didn't have a card, and so they didn't have the option of registering their food purchases. *And isn't choice what our culture is really all about*, we'll be told. People are at the mercy of outdated stores that do not have the infrastructure to implement shopper cards, so we need congressional funding to help all stores avail themselves of this lifesaving technology. And of course at first it will be optional. And taxpayer-funded.

As soon as most people are using the voluntary program, those few who don't will begin to be assailed as bad parents. What? You're buying food and not registering it in the recall database? Your kid could die! Once 90 percent of the people are participating (and by the way, over 75 percent of people now participate in grocery registration programs) you can simply say that those 10 percent who don't are putting their children at risk. They are un-American. They don't care. It means we need a law that says, "You cannot buy food unless you identify yourself. We want to know what you eat. We want to know who you are. We want to know where you live and how to contact you." Buying food anonymously will be a crime.

That was my prediction.

Then a couple of days ago I got a call from an AP reporter who said, "I've heard you're against supermarket loyalty cards. But how could you argue against using them to do recalls of mad cow infected beef?" It turns out there is a lawsuit pending in Seattle on exactly that—a family is suing a huge grocery chain saying it should use its frequent shopper card database for product recalls. And so it begins.

My answer? I told the reporter the same thing I said about the baby-snatching scenario: Those in power create the mess, and then they expect us to sacrifice our privacy to "solve" it. Why is there mad cow disease in this country? What kinds of practices happen on factory farms that lead to the production of toxic, disease-laden beef? Why should I sacrifice my ability to purchase food anonymously so they can continue these hideous industry practices? If I don't solve their mess I somehow become un-American, unpatriotic, unhelpful, unsomething.

Okay, sure, I'm fine with them registering every morsel I eat. And while they're at it, they can stick a camera in my bedroom. I've got nothing to hide, right?

You see this over and over and over.

Remember that article I mentioned about privacy advocates having strange bedfellows, that we're somehow in league with criminals? Who are the real criminals out there today? You want to talk criminals, let's talk about the people and organizations we're up against.

DJ: Let's go back to where we're headed.

KA: To sum all this up, where we're headed without drastic change is total draconian control, under extremely centralized authoritarian power that will probably be global. That's the endpoint if we're not careful. And we now have the technological tools to where the power being sought is available.

DJ: We don't, actually.

KA: We as individuals may not, but as a species we have created immense amounts of power. And once power has been created, the bad guys tend to seek it out to further their goals of amassing wealth and controlling others. To understand the siren call of power, think of the ring in the *Lord of the Rings*. Once the ring is out there, it beckons almost irresistibly. It can be so compelling that even good people have to stay away from it to keep from being corrupted.

But we can resist the abuse of power and change the system. It's certainly been done before. Throughout history people have had to periodically wrest power out of the hands of the corrupt to get their society back on track.

ROBERT McCHESNEY

Interview conducted on
September 8, 1999, at his home
in Madison, Wisconsin.

F or nearly three decades, Robert McChesney has been a modern Paul Revere raising an alarm about the growing domination of the media by giant firms and special interests. There are many sharp academic critics of our corporate media system, but McChesney stands out because of his straightforward writing style and populist commitment to democracy and social change.

What does it mean for democracy, McChesney asks, when a small elite determines the information the rest of us receive about the world? Though every new technology—from radio to television to the Internet—has held out the promise of increased democratization, in the end it's those in control of the medium who have determined what stories get told. Even in the more freewheeling world of the Internet, most actual journalism circulated on the Web is still produced by newspapers. Since this interview, things are much worse—the big corporate newspapers have collapsed, and haven't been replaced with anything offering even that pitiful level of journalism.

In other words: freedom of the press belongs to the person who owns one.

Before earning his PhD in communications from the University of Washington, McChesney worked as a sports writer, published a weekly newspaper, and cofounded the Seattle rock magazine *The Rocket*. He now teaches at the University of Illinois at Urbana-Champaign, where he is a professor in the Institute of Communications Research. His work is primarily concerned with what he calls "the contradiction between a for-profit, highly concentrated, advertising-saturated, corporate media system and the communications requirements of a democratic society."

McChesney is the author or editor of seven books. His tour de force *Rich Media, Poor Democracy: Communication Politics in Dubious Times* (The New Press) earned accolades from, among others, Ralph Nader, Barbara Ehrenreich, and Bill Moyers, who said, "If Thomas Paine were around, he would have written this book." McChesney's other books include *Corporate Media and the Threat to Democracy* (Seven Stories Press); *Global Media: The Missionaries of Corporate Capitalism* (Cassell Academic), with Edward S. Herman; and most recently, *The Death and Life of American Journalism* (Nation Books), with John Nichols. McChesney was also co-editor of the *Monthly Review*, an independent socialist magazine founded in 1949.

I first met Robert McChesney through John Stauber—critic of the public relations industry and editor of the journal *PR Watch*—who invited me to a party at McChesney's home in Madison, Wisconsin. A longtime fan of McChesney's work, I eagerly accepted.

Radicals of every stripe were in attendance. Walking from room to room, I overheard conversations about everything from the role of the media in maintaining current social structures to a really good recipe for banana bread. When I met McChesney, I discovered him to be a big man, warm and self-effacing. I also got to talk to his wife, Inger Stole, an intelligent woman with a strong Norwegian accent.

At the end of the evening, I mentioned to McChesney that I would like to interview him someday. His response was easy and accommodating, and we quickly set a date. I later returned to Madison, and we talked through the hot afternoon in his living room, moving upstairs when one of his daughters needed the space to do her homework.

Derrick Jensen: We hear over and over that the United States has the freest press in the world.

Robert McChesney: Yes, we're told that a private, commercial press system is innately American and democratic, and that, in fact, it's the only true free press system. We internalize this notion early on. It's not a debatable point in our society. The problem, however, is that the type of media system we have today bears almost no resemblance to the type glorified in that mythology, where anyone who wants to can start a newspaper; where if you've got something to say, you can stand up and say it, and you can't be censored. It's true, you can stand on a street corner and state your opinion more or less without fear, but it's also true that, unless you're a billionaire, you won't be able to reach any sort of mass audience, because that's what kind of money it takes to run a major media outlet, like a television network or a film studio.

The way the media giants—the handful of companies that own and operate our media system—present the case to us, you'd think our current media monopoly is divinely ordained, as if Moses handed a tablet to Thomas Jefferson, who handed it to Abe Lincoln, who handed it to Rupert Murdoch. But the media system we have today is purely a twentieth-century phenomenon, quite unlike the one that existed in the first hundred-plus years of the republic. And in most respects, it's diametrically opposed to the type of media system we had at the time the First Amendment to the Constitution was adopted in 1791.

For the first couple of American generations, our media were largely partisan, closely linked to the political process, not especially profitable, and mostly noncommercial. Newspapers in those days were always connected to political parties and factions. You needed your own newspaper in order to be a political force. The whole reason you published one was to convince people to share your political ideas—a completely different purpose from the commercial logic that rules today's media.

Thomas Jefferson and like-minded individuals included freedom of the press in the First Amendment because they knew that if the party in power were able to outlaw dissident newspapers, it could essentially abolish any dissent whatsoever. And, just as Jefferson had foreseen, in the late 1790s President John Adams and the significantly antidemocratic Federalists who supported him tried to purge many of the radical newspaper editors in the country by means of the Alien and Sedition Acts. So the First Amendment wasn't something the Founders dreamed up in order to protect Philip Morris investors two hundred years later. They had a very real, immediate political cause: the survival of democracy.

Another difference between the press at the time of the nation's founding and the press today is that, prior to the twentieth century, the person who owned the newspaper or magazine was always the editor. And the owner-editors usually didn't start the paper to make money, but to spread ideas. The business aspect was just to put food on the table and to allow the press to continue. Our mythology of the "bulldog press" is built on this notion of crusading owner-editors who print the news as they see it, special interests be damned. But by the twentieth century, that standard of owner-editor had pretty much disappeared, and the real power had passed over to the shareholders and corporate managers. These people have the First Amendment rights to hire and fire editors and do as they please, but they have no more interest in politics or democracy than people in the shoe business. They're just out to make money. So in today's media, the power is purely in the hands of commercial interests. Reporters and editors have no power except that which they're granted by the owners.

DJ: It seems to me that investors and managers in the newspaper business— or the shoe business, or any other business—have a distinct interest in politics insofar as it affects their bottom line.

RM: What I mean is that the owners of the media today don't have an intrinsic political affiliation. If you started a newspaper in 1803, you were a Federalist or a Democrat or had some other partisan political agenda driving you. The idea of making huge profits from a newspaper would have been unlikely. But today the primary goal is to make as much money as possible.

DJ: Yet, around the start of the twentieth century, historian and writer Henry Adams said, "The press is the hired agent of a monied system, set up for no other reason than to tell lies where the interests are concerned."

RM: Exactly. By then, the purpose of the newspaper had already changed. The years between the Civil War and World War I saw the transition from political to commercial newspapers, which was part of a larger transition toward commercialization of the culture. Around the 1880s, people began to see that you could make real money running a newspaper. But despite increasing commercialization, the press in the late nineteenth century was still largely a competitive arena. In 1870, in any major city in the U.S., you'd have a number of newspapers to choose from, representing a wide range of political opinions. And if you didn't like any of them, you could always start your own; it didn't cost that much.

But over time—especially as advertising became an important source of revenue—the number of newspapers began to diminish, and it became more difficult to start one. By the turn of the century, most smaller American cities had become one-newspaper towns. Even the larger cities had only three or four dailies. The very largest cities, like New York, still had eight or nine dailies until the 1940s and 1950s, when the number was cut down to three, where it remains today.

So what happens to journalism if you've got only one newspaper in town, and that newspaper gets most of its money from advertisers? For one thing, the newspaper can't be highly partisan, because it would antagonize a significant percentage of its readership, and that would be bad for business. Advertisers, of course, want as large a market share as possible, so owners must try to sell as many copies as possible. Also, as papers have gotten bigger, the owners have gotten wealthier, and it has become less likely that their opinions will go against the interests of the rich.

This trajectory has been the spawning ground for the modern notion of professional, "objective" journalism. In order to maximize market share, newspapers have had to avoid pissing people off, so they created the essentially fictional idea that their editorial content isn't controlled by the owners and advertisers but by journalists with professional standards of neutrality. The idea is to make capitalist, advertising-supported media seem—at least superficially— to be an objective source of news. But that's a myth based on the notion that journalists can act independently of owners and advertisers.

The reality is that reporters knew from the start not to trash advertisers and to always take care of the owners' interests. But, more important, the values of commercialism were smuggled in and internalized, and they have increasingly permeated professional journalism ever since. For example, why are crime stories always considered news, even when there's no specific public issue raised by them? The primary reason is that crime sells newspapers. Because such scare stories are commercially viable, they have become, almost by default, good journalism. But there is nothing inherent in stories about crime and violence that makes them newsworthy outside of the communities where the crimes occur.

Another problem is that professional journalism relies heavily on official sources. Reporters have to talk to the White House press secretary, the cop on the beat, the army general. What those people say is news. Their perspectives are automatically legitimate. But if you talk to prisoners, strikers, the homeless, or protesters, you have to paint their perspectives as unreliable, or else you've become an advocate and are no longer a "neutral" professional journalist. This reliance on official sources gives the news an inherently conservative cast and gives those in power tremendous influence over defining what is or isn't news. This is precisely the opposite of what a functioning democracy needs, which is a ruthless accounting of the powers that be.

DJ: I can't tell you how many environmental reporters I've seen get canned or sent to cover "community activities" because they've become "too close to the issues."

RM: You'll notice that doesn't happen on the business beat. There, getting close to your subject is simply "cultivating your sources."

The state of journalism today is woeful, and exactly what you'd expect in a media system owned by a handful of huge firms controlled by some of the wealthiest individuals in the world. They make billions providing a product that serves the needs of the two hundred largest advertisers—essentially, the largest corporations in the world. And whom do these advertisers want to reach? The richest segment of the population. So the news media are pitched almost exclusively to this demographic group. Thus, it's considered normal for a paper to print eight pages of business news and zero on labor. Imagine what an anomaly it would be if you had a newspaper that contained eight pages on labor issues and none on business and gave lots of sympathetic coverage to strikes and rallies. People would say, "What the hell's going on here? Who's running this newspaper?"

Yet, as recently as the 1940s, it was standard for every midsize or larger U.S. daily to have a full-time labor beat reporter. In cities like Detroit or Chicago or Milwaukee, there would be several. It's been estimated that there were more than a thousand full-time labor reporters and editors at daily newspapers in the forties. So labor issues were covered. When a strike took place, a reporter would talk to union members and find out what they were thinking and doing. The 1937 sit-down strike in Flint, Michigan, which led to the creation of the United Auto Workers union, was front-page news in every paper in the country. Even the *Chicago Tribune*, which was semi-fascist under Colonel McCormick, covered the Flint strike on its front page; it trashed the strikers, but at least its readers knew there was a strike going on.

Do you know how many full-time labor beat reporters there are in U.S. daily newspapers today? Four, at most. The position has been all but eliminated. Even in Detroit—the center of the American labor movement in the twentieth century—the last full-time labor beat reporter was laid off shortly after owners broke the union at the city's two newspapers. In the same year, those papers added fifteen new reporters to cover mall expansions and other "crucial" stories in the suburbs.

This means we have no coverage of labor news in our press, except in those rare cases where the papers absolutely can't avoid paying attention. So if you're a working-class person who's interested in working-class issues—which describes the bulk of the population—our media's news coverage is irrelevant to you. Proof of this came in 1989, when the largest sit-down strike in fifty years took place. Do you know where?

DJ: I've got no clue.

RM: How would you? It wasn't covered. It was a mineworkers' strike in Pittstown, Virginia. And the strikers won, too. But average Americans probably know less about it than they do about Greek philosophy—and certainly less than they do about the Dow Jones index. The only significant national coverage of the Pittstown strike came when some striking Soviet coal miners traveled from Siberia to show solidarity with their brothers and sisters in western Virginia. Finally, *The New York Times* decided to cover that.

DJ: What little coverage I have seen of strikes is universally negative.

RM: That's because strikers are a thorn in the side of society's rightful rulers: the investing class. Our media system is a firm believer in the idea that big business should run society and everyone else should do what's best for big business.

DJ: To what degree do you think most journalists and journalism professors are aware that they're servants to power?

RM: Part of the function of professional standards in journalism (and I suspect it works similarly in other professions) is to make journalists oblivious to the sort of compromises they must constantly make. The point is to make journalists think they're just being responsible and following ethical codes. And journalists have bought into this ideology to such a degree that, especially in the last thirty years, they have been fiercely resistant to any criticism of our media system.

In the last five years, however, I've noticed a major shift in this regard. I used to be a freelance journalist, reporter, and magazine publisher, until I went back to graduate school in 1983. I still periodically see my journalist friends, and I give them my radical critique of the news media and how they serve the interests of the rich and powerful. Throughout the 1980s, my friends would respond: "Bob, you don't know what you're talking about anymore. It's not as bad as all that. You've completely lost touch." Now, when I offer the same critique, my friends say, "Bob, you don't know what you're talking about. You're completely out of touch. It's much worse than you think."

There's been a demoralizing crisis of confidence among thoughtful journalists. You can see it in all the books by ex-journalists lamenting the collapse of their profession under commercial and corporate pressure. The upside of this is that it's made people listen to criticism of our media system.

DJ: But do you actually think some editors and reporters consciously ignore stories and lie to serve the ruling class?

RM: I would compare how our system works to the old Soviet press before glasnost. If you'd gone into a newsroom of Pravda in 1975, you wouldn't have seen KGB guards with guns aimed at the editors' heads, forcing them to stick to the party line. By the time those journalists got to the top of their profession—

the equivalent of working for *The New York Times* or *The Washington Post*—they'd already internalized the values of their society, meaning they believed that what was good for the Communist Party was good for their society. If a story came along that challenged that presumption, they'd instantly dismiss it. No one had to instruct them to do that, because any journalists who had a problem with the Soviet system had been weeded out long before then. If you published an article or two that was critical of the Communist Party, you were likely sent to sell classified ads in Uzbekistan.

And the same thing happens in our media system. By the time you get to *The New York Times* newsroom, you've internalized the values of the ruling class. So when a war comes along in, say, Kosovo, you don't ask such rational questions as "What gives the U.S. the right to invade any country it wants, for any reason it chooses?" or "Why do no other countries have this right?" Instead, you simply assume that the U.S. can do whatever it wants.

Now if, say, Iraq had invaded Yugoslavia, you would have been highly critical of Iraq. And if Iraq had responded, "Well, we've got our own military alliance, just like your NATO. It's called IRAQO, and the invasion is justified because IRAQO voted to do it," our reporters and editors would have laughed and called it a fraud. Yet when Clinton did the same thing, it was' perfectly reasonable.

DJ: Whenever I write for big, commercial magazines, I become discouraged. They go through what I've written and extract the teeth, then go through again to make sure they didn't miss any the first time around. The final result says nothing, offends no one, and has neither substance nor style.

RM: That's exactly how the process works. Let's say a journalist at *The New York Times* who isn't completely brainwashed gets the crazy idea that she'll study the relationship between the CIA and illegal drugs. Her editors won't come right out and say, "That's nonsense." Rather, they'll say, "OK, Sally, work on that for a while." But then she'll find she's not getting any support, and that the piece is being harshly edited. Still, she'll put all her time, energy, and heart into this piece and call in all her favors with sources, editors, and other writers in the hopes that she can uncover this important story. She'll go way out on a limb personally, emotionally, professionally, politically. And then the story won't run. Or if it does run, the newspaper won't stand behind her, the way the *San Jose Mercury News* didn't stand behind Gary Webb after he reported just such a story. After that, Sally will have to win back favor by doing puff pieces about how great our system is, how stupid protesters are, how greedy strikers are. Over time, she's likely to say, "Why should I beat my head against the wall doing hard work that gets me nowhere, when everyone kisses my behind for quoting politicians and reciting government policies?"

DJ: A line I hear all the time to defend corporate journalism or sensationalistic stories is "We're just giving people what they want."

RM: That's a flawed argument on a number of levels. First, journalists who say they're "giving people what they want" are essentially acknowledging that they're no longer journalists, even by their own standards. The ostensible principle behind journalism is that you give people what they need, not what they want. They need information to help them understand the world and public life. Giving people what they want is the job of the entertainment industry.

Second, it's not even true that they're giving us what we want. Yes, if you're constantly exposed to something, it's easy to develop a taste for it. After a year and a half of the O.J. Simpson trial, I was sort of interested in what Kato Kaelin was doing, but that doesn't mean it was what I wanted. I would bet that if people were exposed on a regular basis to really good, hard-hitting journalism, they'd develop a taste for it, too.

The real reason we get so much coverage of O.J. Simpson, Joey Buttafuoco, and JonBenet Ramsey is that they're extremely inexpensive stories to cover and require no journalistic skill, so media corporations save a ton of money.

Also, these stories never cause trouble with anyone in power, which means the newspapers don't have to worry about losing sources or being sued.

Here's a classic example of journalism by the bottom line: Iowa used to have one of the great American newspapers, the *Des Moines Register*. One reason it was such a great paper is that it had a full-time reporter in each of the state's ninety or so counties. Then, in the mid-1980s, the Register was purchased by the media giant Gannett. The first thing Gannett did to fatten up the bottom line was fire almost all those county reporters. Next, the new owners looked at the Washington, D.C., bureau, where the *Register* had a staff of knowledgeable reporters covering agricultural policies full time. The bureau wasn't bringing in any advertising dollars, however, so they fired just about everyone.

Was Gannett giving the people what they wanted? No, but it's easy for them to make that claim, because after fifteen years without coverage of Iowa counties, if you did a survey of twenty-five-year-old Iowans today, they almost certainly wouldn't say, "I want good coverage of local issues around the state," because they don't even know that's an option.

Media giants don't give people what they want; they give people what's most profitable to produce. Then, because you consume it, they claim that it's what you wanted in the first place. It's an insult to democracy.

DJ: When the Soviet Union collapsed, I kept reading in newspapers that Russia was moving "from communism to democracy." It seemed to me that journalists were routinely substituting the word "democracy" for "capitalism."

RM: To use those two words interchangeably is an ideologically loaded construct, because equating them makes it impossible to discuss the antidemocratic implications of our capitalist society. And if you can't discuss those implications, you can't proceed to the next logical step: taking action to preserve democracy.

DJ: Can capitalism and democracy coexist?

RM: Obviously, societies can be both capitalist and democratic, but there will always be a tremendous tension between the two and limits on one or the other, or both. The greater the power of capitalist forces, the weaker the democratic values.

To have a viable, working democracy, you need three things. First, people have to be informed on the issues. This means they must be given a range of high-quality information and opinions, along with a ruthless accounting of the powers that be—and the powers that want to be. These are the tools that allow people to engage in debate, make informed decisions, and govern themselves. If you don't have access to those tools—that is, if your media system doesn't make them readily available—your ability to have a genuine, functioning democracy is reduced.

Second, you need to have some measure of political equality. You've got to believe, no matter how poor you are, that you have as much decision-making power in this society as everyone else—even Bill Gates. If you don't believe that, then you don't live in a democracy.

The third thing necessary for democracy to work—really, for any society to work—is a belief that your happiness, your fate, your lot in the world is dependent on your neighbors'. You can't believe that you can have a great life while everyone around you is unhappy or dying. You've got to have faith in community, or else the whole social fabric unravels. Democracy is predicated on such communal beliefs, while capitalism promotes economic inequality and the individual fight for survival. Its motto is "Take care of number one. You're competing with everyone else for scarce resources, and if you turn your back, they'll screw you, so you'd better screw them first." Everyone knows this is what capitalism is about, but journalists can't admit it, because that wouldn't be in the interests of their employers.

DJ: I've heard about studies suggesting that the more you watch television news, the less you know. How does that work?

RM: Danny Schechter wrote a book called *The More You Watch, the Less You Know* (Seven Stories Press). The book's title refers to a number of surveys showing that the people who consume the most commercial TV news know the least about the subjects covered in those newscasts. The most famous study was done during the Gulf War, in 1991. Three University of Massachusetts social scientists found that people who watched the most CNN coverage of the war knew the least about who the participants were, what the different political positions were, and so on. Also—and this is very frightening—they were the most likely to support U.S. government policy.

One reason these findings are troubling is that they match the plan laid out by Joseph Goebbels in Nazi Germany during the 1930s. His goal for the Nazi media was that the more people consumed of it, the less they would understand the issues, and the more they would support Nazi policies. So our so-called free press produces the same type of results that Goebbels—a man with profound contempt for both democracy and public discourse—was trying to produce in Germany. Another of Goebbels's theories was that, rather than inundate the media with heavy-handed political messages, it was better to give people lots of light entertainment, which he felt made much more effective propaganda. And in our own media today, there is little serious drama to be found. A good mystery is about as close as you can get.

There's more. Goebbels instructed the German media to give the illusion of diversity while making sure that every single program contained the same underlying message. That's an accurate description of our cable television and magazine racks today: seemingly diverse, until you look below the surface.

In effect, our propaganda system is much better than anything Goebbels dreamed up, because it has the illusion of freedom. If you disagreed with the government in Nazi Germany, you got locked up and maybe even executed, so it was apparent that you were living in a repressive society. Here in the U.S., you can blow off steam with a rant on some community radio station or by writing for some fanzine that eight people read, and then you're supposed to shut up and be happy because it proves we have a "free" press. But the dominant system remains highly repressive and undemocratic.

In many respects, we have the greatest propaganda system in human history, much superior to the Soviet or Nazi systems, because our system delivers the message that, if you don't like it, it's your own fault. That's the primary message in our society: if you're not a success, it's your fault. If you're in prison, it's your fault. If you're not happy, it's your fault. It's never the fault of our flawed system. The preservers of the status quo do not want that idea to enter our minds.

DJ: Let's get back to "the more you watch, the less you know." I still don't understand how that works.

RM: Basically, it means that the coverage is so skewed toward the "official" version that you never learn anything of critical importance. So the more you consume—the more you're spoon-fed the party line—the less you're able to engage the difficult questions.

Take Kosovo, for example: If you watch a lot of mainstream news, instead of being able to provide a rudimentary explanation of why the different factions acted the way they did, you're more likely to know only that "They're bad guys. They broke the law, so now we have to punish them." The basic lesson we learn over and over from TV newscasts is that we're the good guys who must deal with all the bad people around the world—people our leaders fortunately identify for us before taking them out.

DJ: All of this goes hand in hand with the near-total silence in the press concerning our appalling military spending.

RM: Even when reporters still had some autonomy from owners and advertisers, certain issues were completely off-limits. And those tended to be issues of critical importance to the ruling class, the one-half of 1 percent who own much of the stock. If the members of the ruling class are in agreement on an issue, debate on it is off-limits for the rest of us. Only if they disagree—or, more often, if an issue is irrelevant to their control of society—is it fair game for journalists and the public. So whether the U.S. has an innate right to invade other countries is off-limits, because maintaining that "right" is crucial to protecting our business interests overseas. It's not in the popular interest, but it's imperative to big business that the U.S. have the ability to overthrow any government it chooses. Even those members of the ruling class who have been opposed to various wars—and there are some—never oppose our innate right to invade whenever we want; they oppose only specific military actions.

The elite is divided on some issues, and those are the ones we get to talk about. And then there are the issues that are irrelevant to the elite's control of society: abortion, gay rights, and so on. This doesn't mean these aren't important issues—just that they aren't important to the ruling class.

Now, you were asking about military spending. That's the one form of government spending that offends no one at the top. Any other form of government spending is subject to at least some skewed form of debate: "Do we really need to spend all that money on healthcare and education? And surely we shouldn't be spending all that money on poor people." But military spending is basically massive corporate welfare for the industrial sector. Many people in that top one-half of 1 percent benefit from it directly by owning stock in Lockheed Martin, Boeing, or some other military contractor. The rest would rather see the money go to the military than elsewhere. If it went toward mass transportation, for example, it would hurt the car companies and the oil companies. The products of military spending don't compete with any other products in the market. What's more, if the planes and bombs are used, they'll be used to toss out a government that's unfriendly to U.S. business interests. And even if there's a major war, none of the richest kids will have to fight, because in this country, rich people are, for all intents and purposes, excused from military service.

DJ: There's a quote dating from the Civil War that sums this up perfectly. Judge Thomas Mellon, an extremely wealthy man, wrote to his son, who was feeling guilty for buying his way out of the army: "In time you will understand and believe that a man may be a patriot without risking his own life or sacrificing his health. There are plenty of other lives less valuable."

RM: Some extraordinary studies have been done documenting the degree to which the poor alone fought the Vietnam War. If you look at the graduating classes of all the Ivy League universities and other elite private universities during the Vietnam War era—from 1960 to 1975—you find that out of that couple of hundred thousand people, something like five or ten, were killed in Vietnam. But in South Boston, an Irish working-class neighborhood, there were maybe a hundred kids within a twenty-square-block area who died. That's another subject we can't talk about in the media: that poor kids fought that war. And black kids. And, of course, Vietnamese kids. But upper-middle-class white kids by and large didn't fight.

One reason Bill Clinton didn't get trashed for avoiding the draft is because he was just doing the same thing almost every other middle-class kid did. If you had money, there were ways to get out of serving. I'm sure you've heard that Al Gore served in Vietnam, but that was only because his father was running for reelection in Tennessee and was being called a liberal. Gore went to prove his dad was a patriot, but of course he got a cushy desk job. His life was never in danger. You know the song "Fortunate Son," by Creedence Clearwater Revival? Remember the line "I ain't no senator's son"? They were protesting the fact that Gore was over there serving cocktails to officers while poor kids were dying.

This may seem to be off the subject of the media, but it's crucial, because the idea of a "classless" society is the single biggest lie of our time. We're not allowed to talk about the fact that we live in a class-based society.

DJ: We've been discussing newspapers so far, but the conglomerates that control the media extend far beyond print media.

RM: In all the companies that dominate the news media, journalism is rarely more than half of their activities, and often—as in the case of the News Corporation, Disney, or Time Warner—news represents less than 10 percent of their activities and revenues.

If you look back at the U.S. media industry in the 1940s and 1950s, you'll see seven major media sectors: newspapers, radio, movies, books, magazines, music, and the brand new medium of television. Each of those sectors was dominated by anywhere from a handful to a couple of dozen companies. With newspapers, it was maybe twenty-five large companies. And these sectors tended to be distinct. In other words, big newspaper companies didn't also own film studios or TV networks.

Two things have happened in the last fifty years. First, there has been a tremendous consolidation within each sector, so instead of twenty-five or thirty newspaper chains, we've now got five or six huge newspaper companies. And instead of fifteen or twenty big music companies, today only four companies sell 87 percent of the music in the U.S. More significant, however, has been the rise of the media conglomerate, a media company that owns businesses in not just one sector, but several. If you look at the holdings of the three largest media companies in the U.S. today—Time Warner, Disney, and Viacom—you find that each is among the biggest players in six or seven different media sectors.

Time Warner, for example, is the second-largest cable TV provider and owns by far the most channels, including CNN, TNT, TBS, Court TV, HBO, and Cinemax. It has two big film studios—Warner Brothers and New Line—and is the largest magazine publisher in the U.S., producing *Time*, *People*, *Sports Illustrated*, *Fortune*, and many others. Time Warner is also a big book publisher and one of the three or four largest music companies. Let's not forget it also owns 150 retail stores and several amusement parks.

DJ: Why is this consolidation taking place now?

RM: If you believe another myth of our media system, domination by giant corporations is inevitable, some sort of natural selection. Of course, that's nonsense. The reason this overwhelming consolidation is taking place now is that our antitrust regulations have been gutted. Until fairly recently, regulations prevented linkage of broadcast companies with newspapers and other types of media. Moreover, there were strict regulations that prevented those who owned TV stations and networks from producing the shows that appeared on them. All those regulations have now been tossed out or weakened, making these media giants possible. And the profit from these interlinked parts is much greater than from the sum of each part working separately, because they all work together instead of competing with each other.

For example, in 1994, Disney made a children's movie called *The Lion King*. Since I have a young daughter, I saw it more than a dozen times. It grossed about $700 million at the box office worldwide. Disney got to keep about half of that, while theater owners got the other half. That's $350 million in revenues. But look at all the other things Disney can do with *The Lion King* besides theatrical distribution. They can put it on their Disney Channel, and on ABC, too. They can make *Lion King* spinoffs and sequels. They've produced all sorts of *Lion King* merchandise to sell in their 660 Disney stores around the world, not to mention other retail outlets. They can make amusement park rides, CD-ROMs, books, and soundtracks from the movie. The possibilities are endless. By the time it's all counted, Disney has made probably more than a billion dollars in profit on *The Lion King*. In fact, Disney can make a movie that flops at the box office and still make a profit. This means that if you're trying to enter the animated film business, you'd better have the same merchandising arsenal, or you won't be able to compete.

The possibility of in-house promotion actually makes the market even more slanted toward the big conglomerates. When Viacom-owned Paramount Pictures made a movie from the children's show *Rugrats*, it could advertise the movie incessantly on Nickelodeon, MTV, and all the other media outlets Viacom owns, whereas an independent filmmaker who made the same movie would have had to pay a fortune for that advertising. So Viacom spent $10 million on that movie and cleared something like $80 or $90 million just in box office revenues, and that's before they even started counting all the other profits.

DJ: I think it's pretty clear what's wrong with having just a half-dozen companies deliver almost all the news, but what's wrong with having a half-dozen companies make all the movies? Aren't movies just entertainment?

RM: First of all, these few companies have tremendous control over what movies can be made. The movies that get produced are the ones that will make the most money and don't rock the ideological boat. Hollywood history is replete with stories of talented people who've fought hard and gotten good movies made, but for every good movie that's released, dozens more are cranked out purely to make a profit.

Second, and probably more important, is that the films themselves have in some ways become almost incidental to the industry. Many films are now just part of a broader marketing scheme to sell "brands." A good example is the movie *Space Jam*, which came out several years ago, starring Michael Jordan and Bugs Bunny. Basically, Time Warner didn't even care whether anyone went to see the movie in the theater, because they'd already figured out how to make millions from selling cups, mugs, t-shirts, sweatpants, and other merchandise with images of Michael Jordan and Bugs Bunny affixed to it. They've turned our entire media system into a commercial. Any notion of integrity, of separating the creative product from the commercial, is collapsing under the weight of these money hungry giants.

These days, the only way a piece with a powerful political message can get made is if a big star is willing to use all of her or his influence to force it through.

This takes enormous determination and sacrifice, and afterward the star will have to go back and do more insipid moneymakers to build up her or his stock again. Take *Bulworth*, a great movie with a great message. If it hadn't been for Warren Beatty, the script wouldn't have gotten past the intern at the front door. And now, because that movie didn't make as much money as the studio wanted, Beatty will probably have a harder time making another political movie. As with journalists, it doesn't take long for an actor or director with a strong egalitarian vision to get beaten down.

DJ: But even with all the rewards out there for going with the flow, there are still a lot of people who are fighting against it.

RM: That's right. We don't have to accept this system as a given. It exists simply because our laws created it—with no public participation in the process—and we have a right and a duty to change those laws, to go back and create a media system that serves democracy. Why should we allow Wall Street and Madison Avenue to turn us upside down, shake the money out of our pants, and then drop us and move on to the next target audience?

Even in today's depoliticized society, there's an increasing interest in these issues. Fifteen years ago, I'd say these things, and people would look at me as if I were anti-American, but nowadays people understand that the situation has gotten out of hand. We're talking about the commercial carpet-bombing of our brains in a way that was unthinkable twenty-five or thirty years ago. Our society talks about how much it loves kids, yet we subject our children to twenty-four-hour cable channels that bombard them with advertisements. The average American kid today sees maybe thirty thousand commercials a year. And now these Madison Avenue hotshots are marketing to two-year-olds. They've got scientific plans on how to get into preschoolers' heads. We have no idea what this will do to the next generation, but the hotshots don't care. They're just out to make money.

Some exciting organizing has already begun to battle this. Communities around the country are pressuring their local TV news shows to stop depending on violence and racist crime reporting and actually practice journalism that will help their communities. Some working-class and minority neighborhoods are fighting to get billboards taken down. It's startling for a middle-class person to go into a poor neighborhood and see the booze and cigarette ads everywhere.

On the national level, there are movements to establish nonprofit, noncommercial public broadcasting with enough money to develop great programming without corporate support. Another important effort is to try to require commercial broadcasters to perform real public service in exchange for their licenses. Probably the largest sector of corporate welfare—arguably even greater than the military budget—has been the government's gift of the public airwaves to corporations. They don't pay a penny for the broadcast rights that have allowed them to build these massive companies. Why not make it a condition of having a broadcast license that they accept no political advertising during electoral campaigns? Expensive television ads have turned our electoral politics into a sick joke. Getting rid of them would eliminate more than half the money spent on campaigns and make it easier for someone who's neither a billionaire nor beholden to billionaires to get involved in politics. And why not make it illegal for broadcasters to advertise to kids under twelve? That's already the case in Sweden, and may soon be throughout Europe.

Finally, we need viable antitrust regulations in this country. We have to work to break up these huge media giants. We can't allow this much cultural power to rest with such a small number of institutions.

The first step is to say, "We don't have to accept this. We can change it." We should refuse to be defined as consumers. We are citizens, active participants in our own communities. The biggest fear the media giants have is that the public will find out what's going on and get involved. That's why they bend over backward to sneak laws through in Washington with no public discussion. And when news accidentally does get out, they put their top PR people on it to drown out any reasoned debate and discussion. They're afraid that, once the public really understands how our media system works, we will demand change. They don't want us involved in politics, so they do everything in their power to keep us on the couch in front of the TV. But they can't hide forever the fact that the power really is ours, if we choose to use it.

ABOUT FLASHPOINT PRESS

Flashpoint Press was founded by Derrick Jensen to ignite a resistance movement. Our planet is under serious threat from industrial civilization, with its consumption of biotic communities, production of greenhouse gases and environmental toxins, and destruction of human rights and human-scale cultures around the globe. This system will not stop voluntarily, and it cannot be reformed.

Flashpoint Press believes that the Left has severely limited its strategic thinking, by insisting on education, lifestyle change and techno-fixes as the only viable and ethical options. None of these responses can address the scale of the emergency now facing our planet. We need both a serious resistance movement and a supporting culture of resistance that can inspire and protect frontline activists. Flashpoint embraces the necessity of all levels of action, from cultural work to militant confrontation. We also intend to win.

FLASHPOINT PRESS
CRESCENT CITY, CALIFORNIA

ABOUT DERRICK JENSEN

Hailed as the philosopher poet of the ecological movement, Derrick Jensen is the widely acclaimed author of *Endgame*, *A Language Older Than Words*, and *The Culture of Make Believe* among many others. Jensen's writing has been described as "breaking and mending the reader's heart" (*Publishers Weekly*). His books with PM include: *How Shall I Live My Life?: On Liberating the Earth from Civilization* and the novels *Songs of the Dead* and *Lives Less Valuable*.

Author, teacher, activist, and leading voice of uncompromising dissent, he regularly stirs auditoriums across the country with revolutionary spirit. Jensen holds a degree in mineral engineering physics from the Colorado School of Mines, and has taught at Eastern Washington University and Pelican Bay Prison. He lives in Crescent City, California.

PO Box 23912
Oakland, CA 94623
www.pmpress.org

PM Press was founded at the end of 2007 by a small collection of folks with decades of publishing, media, and organizing experience. PM co-founder Ramsey Kanaan started AK Press as a young teenager in Scotland almost 30 years ago and, together with his fellow PM Press co-conspirators, has published and distributed hundreds of books, pamphlets, CDs, and DVDs. Members of PM have founded enduring book fairs, spearheaded victorious tenant organizing campaigns, and worked closely with bookstores, academic conferences, and even rock bands to deliver political and challenging ideas to all walks of life. We're old enough to know what we're doing and young enough to know what's at stake.

We seek to create radical and stimulating fiction and non-fiction books, pamphlets, t-shirts, visual and audio materials to entertain, educate and inspire you. We aim to distribute these through every available channel with every available technology - whether that means you are seeing anarchist classics at our bookfair stalls; reading our latest vegan cookbook at the café; downloading geeky fiction e-books; or digging new music and timely videos from our website.

PM Press is always on the lookout for talented and skilled volunteers, artists, activists and writers to work with. If you have a great idea for a project or can contribute in some way, please get in touch.

FRIENDS OF PM PRESS

These are indisputably momentous times – the financial system is melting down globally and the Empire is stumbling. Now more than ever there is a vital need for radical ideas.

In the year since its founding – and on a mere shoestring – PM Press has risen to the formidable challenge of publishing and distributing knowledge and entertainment for the struggles ahead. With over 75 releases to date, we have published an impressive and stimulating array of literature, art, music, politics, and culture. Using every available medium, we've succeeded in connecting those hungry for ideas and information to those putting them into practice.

Friends of PM allows you to directly help impact, amplify, and revitalize the discourse and actions of radical writers, filmmakers, and artists. It provides us with a stable foundation from which we can build upon our early successes and provides a much-needed subsidy for the materials that can't necessarily pay their own way. You can help make that happen – and receive every new title automatically delivered to your door once a month – by joining as a Friend of PM Press. And, we'll throw in a free T-Shirt when you sign up.

Here are your options:

* $25 a month: Get all books and pamphlets plus 50% discount on all webstore purchases
* $25 a month: Get all CDs and DVDs plus 50% discount on all webstore purchases
* $40 a month: Get all PM Press releases plus 50% discount on all webstore purchases
* $100 a month: Superstar - Everything plus PM merchandise, free downloads, and 50% discount on all webstore purchases

For those who can't afford $25 or more a month, we're introducing Sustainer Rates at $15, $10 and $5. Sustainers get a free PM Press t-shirt and a 50% discount on all purchases from our website.

Your Visa or Mastercard will be billed once a month, until you tell us to stop. Or until our efforts succeed in bringing the revolution around. Or the financial meltdown of Capital makes plastic redundant. Whichever comes first.